# English Unlimited

## B1+ Intermediate
## Self-study Pack (Workbook with DVD-ROM)

Maggie Baigent & Nick Robinson



CAMBRIDGE UNIVERSITY PRESS

CAMBRIDGE UNIVERSITY PRESS
Cambridge, New York, Melbourne, Madrid, Cape Town,
Singapore, São Paulo, Delhi, Tokyo, Mexico City

Cambridge University Press
The Edinburgh Building, Cambridge CB2 8RU, UK

www.cambridge.org
Information on this title: www.cambridge.org/9780521151825



First published 2011
Reprinted 2012

Printed in the United Kingdom at the University Press, Cambridge

*A catalogue record for this publication is available from the British Library*

ISBN 978-0-521-15182-5 Intermediate Self-study Pack (Workbook with DVD-ROM)
ISBN 978-0-521-73989-4 Intermediate Coursebook with e-Portfolio
ISBN 978-0-521-15717-9 Intermediate Teacher's Pack
ISBN 978-0-521-73990-0 Intermediate Class Audio CDs

# Contents

# 1 Media around the world

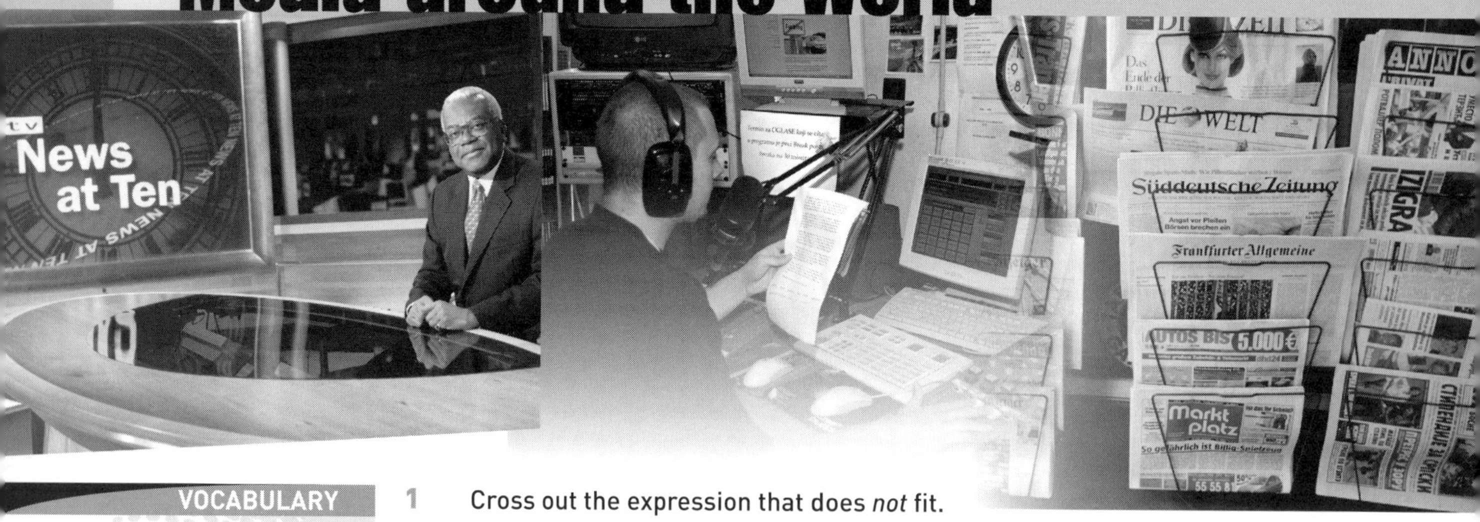


**VOCABULARY**
Habits and preferences

**1 Cross out the expression that does *not* fit.**

1. I can't stand / ~~I'm really into~~ / I hardly ever watch sport on TV. I find it really boring.
2. I don't watch much TV. I'd rather / I prefer to / I used to read a book or listen to the radio.
3. I'm not keen on / I'm a big fan of / I'm really into reality shows. I know they're stupid, but they're really entertaining.
4. When I want to hear the news when I'm working, I tend to / I'll / I hardly ever listen to the radio on the Internet.

**GRAMMAR**
Talking about the present

**2 Complete what Melanie says with the correct form of the verbs in brackets: present simple, present progressive or present perfect simple.**

Melanie, New Zealand

When I lived at home, I used to watch quite a lot of television in the evenings with my mum, but now I [1] *'ve moved* (move) to Auckland and I [2] ____________ (not watch) it much. There are too many other things to do – I [3] ____________ (enjoy) meeting new people and checking out new places at the moment. I [4] ____________ (use) the Internet a lot at work, so when I'm at home I [5] ____________ (prefer) to read or watch a movie. I [6] ____________ (see) some really good films recently – now I don't have to watch the programmes my mum likes!

**3 Complete the questions with the correct form of the verb in brackets.**

1 **A** *Are* you *reading* anything at the moment? (read)
  **B** Only some stuff for work, actually.

2 **A** ____________ you ____________ any TV programmes in English? (watch)
  **B** I sometimes see the news on the BBC or Al Jazeera.

3 **A** ____________ you ____________ the news today? (hear)
  **B** No, what's happened?

4 **A** ____________ you ____________ the same kind of programmes as you used to do? (enjoy)
  **B** Well, I still like documentaries and nature programmes, but I've stopped watching reality shows.

5 **A** ____________ you ____________ any good TV series at the moment? (watch)
  **B** No, there's nothing very interesting on.

6 **A** ____________ you ____________ anything good recently? (read)
  **B** Yes, I read a really good book by someone called Fred Vargas, who's a woman, actually!

**Over to you**

**Write your answers to the six questions, or record them using the DVD-ROM.**

**VOCABULARY**
Talking about facts and information

**4** Complete the words in this advice for young journalists.

http://www.yourmediacareer.org

## TIPS FOR YOUNG JOURNALISTS

Want to be a journalist? Make sure you get the facts right!

✔ Use [1]**re**_liable_______ sources! Get your information from places you can [2]**tr**__________ .

✔ Check those numbers! Don't use [3]**in**__________ data or statistics.

✔ Be honest! People might enjoy gossip or [4]**sc**__________ about famous people, but don't [5]**m**__________ **u**__________ stories – you'll be in big trouble if your story's a [6]**f**__________ .

**VOCABULARY**
Evaluating and recommending

**5** Match the sentence halves.

1 Listening to music on your MP3 player is a great way … _e_
2 If you're doing research, it's a bad idea … ☐
3 The Internet is a good place … ☐
4 Now is a good time … ☐
5 Online newspapers are an easy way … ☐
6 It's a good idea … ☐

a to read different people's opinions.
b to get up-to-date news.
c to start an online magazine.
d to download podcasts of programmes you like, so you can listen to them again.
e to relax when you're travelling.
f to get all your information from just one source, like Wikipedia.

**6** Add *really* to make sentences 1–3 stronger, and *quite* to make sentences 4–6 weaker.

*1 Listening to music on your MP3 player is a* ^*really* *great way to relax when you're travelling.*

**VOCABULARY**
Describing books and TV shows

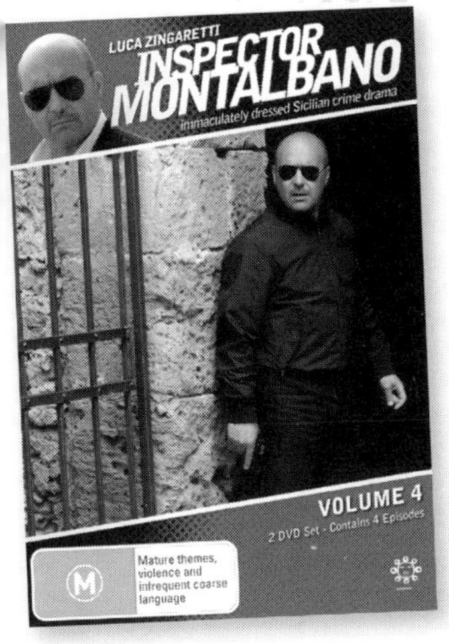


**7** Complete the expressions in bold using the words in the box.

| about | based | ~~called~~ | found | has | looks | really | say | shows | well-known |
|---|---|---|---|---|---|---|---|---|---|

1 **It's by someone** ___*called*___ Andrea Camilleri.
2 **It's** __________ this police detective, Salvo Montalbano.
3 **It** __________ a well-known actor **in it**.
4 **I** __________ **it** quite hard to read.
5 **It** __________ **at** the reality of life in a small town in Sicily.
6 **People** __________ **it's** very realistic.
7 **It's quite a** __________ series.
8 **It's** __________ **on** life in the writer's own town.
9 **Basically, it** __________ **you** the character of this police inspector.
10 **It's a** __________ interesting programme.

**8** Which sentences are about the book? Which are about the TV series? Which can be both?

# MY English

9 **Read what Christine says about learning English through the media and choose the correct way to complete the sentences.**

1 Twenty years ago, Christine used English / Spanish more for her work and free-time activities.
2 Compared with twenty years ago, Christine has more / less contact with English.

I'm from England originally, but I live in Spain with my husband, Ramón. We run a riding school near Bilbao. When I first came here about twenty years ago, I had to learn Spanish fast, as I hardly ever saw or heard English. All films and TV programmes were dubbed in Spanish, there was just one bookshop that had a few, very expensive English books, and I occasionally found an English newspaper or magazine at the station. Now it's totally different – we have a satellite so I can watch English and American TV, films on DVD have the original language, and of course the Internet is brilliant for online papers, radio, podcasts, video clips ... everything! And if I want to read an English book, it's quick and cheap to order online. Brilliant! My kids really enjoy their English lessons, too – their teachers often use stuff from the Internet in class. There's never been a better time to learn English, I think.

## YOUR English

10 **Have you ever used the resources Christine talks about in your English classes? For the things you have used, circle a number: 1 = I didn't like this, 5 = I liked this a lot.**

| | | | | | |
|---|---|---|---|---|---|
| a film, or part of a film | 1 | 2 | 3 | 4 | 5 |
| a TV programme, or part of one | 1 | 2 | 3 | 4 | 5 |
| a book, or part of a book | 1 | 2 | 3 | 4 | 5 |
| an article from a newspaper | 1 | 2 | 3 | 4 | 5 |
| an article from a magazine | 1 | 2 | 3 | 4 | 5 |
| a radio programme, or part of one | 1 | 2 | 3 | 4 | 5 |
| a podcast | 1 | 2 | 3 | 4 | 5 |
| a video clip | 1 | 2 | 3 | 4 | 5 |

11 **How easy is it for you to find these things in English *outside* the classroom? Have you read, watched or listened to any of them? Which did you enjoy the most? Which was the most difficult?**

12 **How much do you agree with Christine that 'there's never been a better time to learn English'?**

# EXPLORE Reading

**13** **Look at this product description for a TV series. What type of programme is it?**

a geography b nature c photography

With a production budget of $25 million, and from the makers of *Blue Planet*, comes the epic story of life on Earth. Five years in production, over 2,000 days in the field, using 40 cameramen in 200 locations, this is the ultimate portrait of our planet.

**14** **Read the main text and complete the product information for the DVD set.**

File Edit View Favorites Tools Help

Address http://www.all-reviews.co.uk/Planet-Earth-DVD

Go Links

| | | | |
|---|---|---|---|
| **Year of release:** | 1 ___________ | **Extra features:** | |
| **Narrator:** | 2 ___________ | • 6 ___________ – short documentaries showing how the programmes were made | |
| **Music by:** | 3 ___________ | • 7 ___________ – experts discuss conservation | |
| **Number of episodes:** | 4 ___________ | | |
| **Length of episodes:** | 5 ___________ | **Number of DVDs in set:** | 8 ___________ |

## Editorial Reviews

Released in 2007, *Planet Earth* is quite simply the greatest nature/wildlife series ever produced. This astonishing 11-part BBC series is brilliantly narrated by Sir David Attenborough and sensibly organised so that each 50-minute episode covers a specific geographical region and/or wildlife habitat (mountains, deserts, forests, etc.) until the entire planet has been magnificently represented by the most astonishing sights and sounds you'll ever experience from home. The first episode serves as an introduction, placing the entire series in context and giving a general overview of what to expect from each episode. The series maintains a consistent emphasis on the urgent need for ongoing conservation, best illustrated by the polar bears, whose behaviour is changing because of global warming. With this harsh reality as subtext, the series proceeds to accentuate the positive, delivering a seemingly endless variety of natural wonders, from the spectacular displays of New Guinea's birds of paradise to a rare encounter with Siberia's nearly-extinct Amur leopards, of which only 30 remain.

Accompanied by majestic orchestral scores by George Fenton, every episode is packed with images so beautiful or so impressive (and so perfectly photographed by the BBC's camera crews) that you'll be speechless. You'll see a seal struggling to out-manoeuvre a great white shark; an awesome night-vision sequence of lions attacking an elephant; the bioluminescent 'vampire squid' of the deep oceans ... these are just a few of countless highlights, masterfully filmed from every angle, with frequent use of super-slow-motion and amazing time-lapse cinematography. The result is a hugely entertaining series that doesn't flinch from the realities of nature (death is a constant presence), and each episode ends with 10-minute 'Planet Earth Diaries' that cover a specific aspect of production.

With so many natural wonders on display, it's only fitting that the final DVD in this five-disc set is *Planet Earth: The Future*, a separate series in which experts discuss conservation and the protection of delicate ecosystems. Now, when the threats of global warming are obvious to all, let's give Sir David the last word, from *Planet Earth*'s final episode: 'We can now destroy or we can protect – the choice is ours.' *Jeff Shannon*

**15** **Are these statements about the series true or false?**

1 Every episode shows many different geographical areas. TRUE / FALSE
2 The series gives evidence that we need to protect the earth. TRUE / FALSE
3 Different filming techniques were used in the series. TRUE / FALSE
4 In *Planet Earth: The Future*, David Attenborough discusses conservation. TRUE / FALSE

**Over to you**

What do you think you would enjoy watching in this DVD?

# 1 Interview Different ways of life

**1** Before you watch, think about these questions. Have you ever been to another place where the ways of behaving were different from your own culture? What kinds of things did you notice?

Inmaculada

Alex

**2** Watch Inmaculada talking about Seville and Alex talking about Marrakesh. Which city do these ways of behaving refer to? Write S or M.

1 people go to each other's houses ☐
2 people don't pay the full price for things ☐
3 people say hello to each other in the street ☐
4 people exchange stories with each other ☐
5 people invite you for tea ☐

**3** Watch Inmaculada again (0:11–1:50). Are these statements true or false?

1 She thinks her neighbours in Seville are more important than family. TRUE / FALSE
2 She is not currently living in Seville. TRUE / FALSE
3 She has a good relationship with her neighbours at the moment. TRUE / FALSE
4 She doesn't like the fact that, in Seville, your neighbours know what you're doing. TRUE / FALSE

**4** Match the sentence halves to complete what Alex says about his experience of Marrakesh. Then watch again (1:54–3:08) to check.

1 What's so famous about Marrakesh ...
2 In Marrakesh, everything that you bought in the market, ...
3 If they told you a price, ...
4 As we got to know them more and more ...
5 We were surprised when ...

a they became more friendly.
b you needed to bargain for it.
c is basically, really, the markets.
d one of the shopkeepers actually invited us.
e you needed basically to knock off 75% of it.

**5** Complete what Inmaculada says about relationships with neighbours. Watch again (0:11–1:50) to check.

close helpful explain know relationship anonymous family business carry on

1 You have a very close ________________ with your neighbours; they are like ________________ .
2 Everybody knows about your ________________ .
3 You live a more ________________ life; you are not as ________________ with your neighbours.
4 I don't ________________ any of my neighbours where I live at the moment.
5 You ________________ with your life and you don't have to ________________ yourself to anybody.
6 It is ________________ to know that if you need help, your neighbour is there.

**6** Complete these extracts from what Alex says about shopping in Marrakesh with correct prepositions. Watch again (1:54–3:08) to check.

- ... markets that sell practically and literally everything, [1]________________ jugs [2]________________ dried foods [3]________________ clothes [4]________________ leather shoes.
- You had to bargain [5]________________ everything, it's slightly different [6]________________ back home.
- It's not just [7]________________ buying the item, more of getting to know the story [8]________________ it.
- People might actually invite you [9]________________ some mint tea.

**7** What ways of life do you think people might find different when they visit your city or country?

## GLOSSARY

**your business** (noun): your private life, the things that you do
**pros and cons** (noun): good things and bad things, advantages and disadvantages
**oppressive** (adjective): not relaxing or pleasant
**claustrophobic** (adjective): If a situation is claustrophobic, it makes you feel you have no freedom.
**bargain** (verb): to discuss the price to pay for something

# 2 Good communication

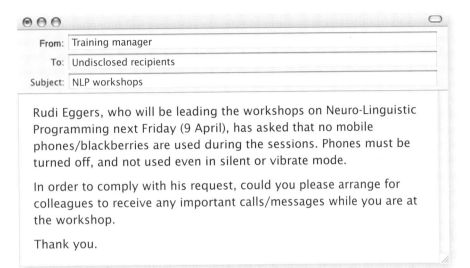

**From:** Training manager
**To:** Undisclosed recipients
**Subject:** NLP workshops

Rudi Eggers, who will be leading the workshops on Neuro-Linguistic Programming next Friday (9 April), has asked that no mobile phones/blackberries are used during the sessions. Phones must be turned off, and not used even in silent or vibrate mode.

In order to comply with his request, could you please arrange for colleagues to receive any important calls/messages while you are at the workshop.

Thank you.

**VOCABULARY**
Expressing opinions

1 **Read the email and complete the expressions in bold in the conversation between two colleagues using the words in the box.**

I'd   no point   people   reckon   say   there's

A Have you seen this email about the NLP workshop?

B Yeah, **I** 1__________ it's a good idea.

A 2__________ **say** it's a stupid idea!

B But **they** 3__________ it's really important to concentrate in NLP, and mobiles can be really distracting.

A Hmm, maybe. I suppose **there's** 4__________ **in** going to the workshop if you don't take it seriously.

B Yes, and **some** 5__________ **say** we use our mobiles too much anyway. 6__________ **no harm in** turning it off for a few hours – it might be quite nice!

**VOCABULARY**
*It's* + adjectives

2 **Complete the people's opinions using the phrases in the box.**

doing the same things   how many   surfing the Net   to answer emails   to keep in touch   to leave your phone   what   when

1. It's important __________ with old friends.
2. It's interesting __________ older people are on Facebook.
3. It's relaxing __________ .
4. It's stressful __________ you have to make phone calls in English.
5. It's boring __________ every day.
6. It's good __________ at home sometimes.
7. It's important __________ immediately.
8. It's surprising __________ people write on Twitter.

**Over to you**

**Do you agree with these opinions? If not, change the adjective to give your opinion.**
*It's difficult to keep in touch with old friends.*

**VOCABULARY**
Using the Internet

**3** **Complete the questions. The same verb is used in each group of questions.**

| | | |
|---|---|---|
| 1 How much time do you *spend* | online?<br>on your favourite site? | |
| 2 Do you regularly ________ | a search engine?<br>an online dictionary? | |
| 3 Do you ________ your own | website?<br>blog?<br>Facebook profile? | |
| 4 Do you ________ | surfing?<br>socialising online? | |
| 5 Do you ________ | blogs?<br>online newspapers? | |
| 6 Do you sometimes ________ | a comment<br>a photo<br>a video | on websites? |

**Over to you**

Write your answers to some of the questions in Exercise 3.

**GRAMMAR**
*will, could, may, might*

**4** **Rewrite the underlined parts of the sentences using the modal verb in brackets.**

1 Perhaps I'll get a new computer next year. (might) *I might get*
2 People say prices are going to be lower then. (will) ________
3 Maybe I won't go to the meeting. (may not) ________
4 Maybe her phone's switched off. (could) ________
5 It's impossible that books will disappear completely. (won't) ________

**VOCABULARY**
Speculating about consequences

**5** **Read the website tips for good non-verbal communication and complete them using the phrases in the box.**

> be able to  it might actually help  it might be good  it will be more difficult  might need to  when  will  will cause  you'll  you'll have to

https://www.body-language.net

## EFFECTIVE COMMUNICATION – WITHOUT WORDS

Even when we are not speaking, our face and body are still communicating. Learn a few basic techniques and you'll [1]________ send the right messages.

Eye contact is one of the most important aspects of body language. It's important to show people we are listening and this [2]________ give them a feeling of warmth [3]________ you are talking. But don't overdo this; too much eye contact [4]________ people to feel uncomfortable.

But if you want to improve your body language, [5]________ think about other aspects, too.

Stand or sit straight; don't let your shoulders fall forward. You might think [6]________ to maintain this posture, but [7]________ you to feel more relaxed.

Don't move your arms, legs or head too much; we tend to move a lot more when we are nervous.

And finally, try to relax, smile, and speak slowly and calmly. Do this, and [8]________ look, sound and feel more confident.

You [9]________ practise some of these tips so they become natural for you; [10]________ to practise with a friend or colleague.

**VOCABULARY**
Expressing probability

6 Use some of the expressions in the box to say how likely you are to do these things in the next 3–5 years.

| definitely | may well | probably | likely | unlikely | more / less likely |
|---|---|---|---|---|---|

*I'm unlikely to move house. I'm more likely to be in the same flat.*

1 I ______________________________ move house.
2 I ______________________________ travel abroad.
3 I ______________________________ find a new job.
4 I ______________________________ take up a new interest or sport.
5 I ______________________________ get married.
6 I ______________________________ make some online friends.
7 I ______________________________ start a new blog.
8 I ______________________________ continue to study English.

## TimeOut

7 Do the quiz. Choose the correct answers.

# ANIMAL COMMUNICATION

How much do you know about 'animal talk'? Try this quiz.

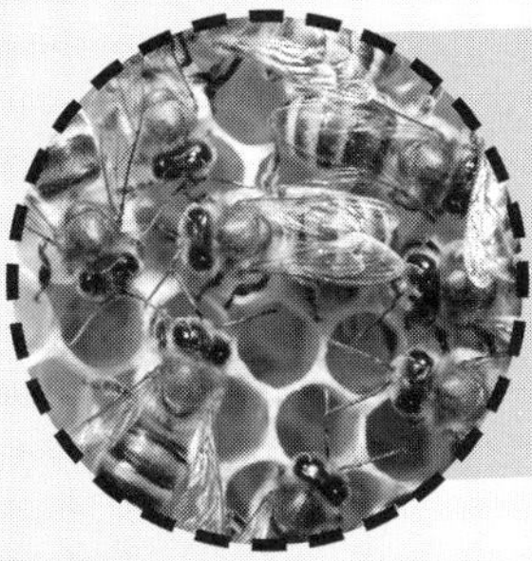

1 Honey bees do a song and dance …
a to tell other bees where food can be found.
b to create a sense of unity in the bee community.

2 North American prairie dogs use 'language' to …
a explain where food can be found.
b identify and describe humans and other animals.

3 Dolphins have their own 'names', which are …
a given to them by their mothers.
b created by the baby dolphins themselves.

4 The songs of humpback whales can last …
a up to twenty minutes.
b up to thirty minutes.

5 Like humans, some birds seem to be 'hardwired' to learn ____________.
a grammar
b music

6 Young vervet monkeys learn to make appropriate alarm calls by …
a being taught and corrected by adult monkeys.
b observing adult monkeys.

# EXPLORE Writing

**8** Read the introduction to a website article. How do you think we can make a good impression when we introduce ourselves online?

http://improveyourprofile.org

Health » Personal Development

**When we meet people in person, first impressions are important. With the Internet expanding our social circle, we have to adapt the way we make our first impressions.**

**9** Match the headings (1–6) with the advice (a–f).

1 Be relevant [d]
2 Don't tell them everything [ ]
3 Be happy [ ]
4 Be brief [ ]
5 Be creative [ ]
6 Check spelling and grammar [ ]

a A quick picture of your life and who you are is all you can write.
b Leave something to talk about later; don't try to put your whole life in your profile.
c Have fun writing your profile and make it interesting to read.
d Include any information that is important to the group you are posting to.
e If you want to make a bad impression, fill your profile with bad spelling and grammar!
f Nobody wants to write to people who make them feel bad; put on your happy face while you write your description.

**10** Read this profile sent to a website for people learning and using English. How far has Mette followed the advice?

1 Do you think she has given a good 'picture of her life'?
2 What other things can she 'talk about later'?
3 How does Mette make her profile interesting to read?
4 Which information is relevant to an ESL (English as a Second Language) group?
5 Can you find three spelling mistakes in Mette's self-description?
6 What things does Mette sound happy and positive about?

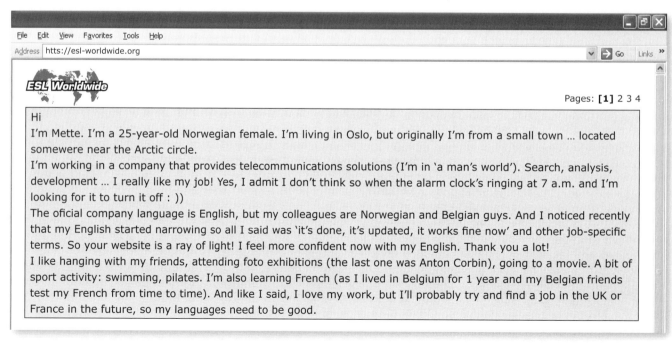

File Edit View Favorites Tools Help
Address https://esl-worldwide.org

ESL Worldwide

Pages: **[1]** 2 3 4

Hi
I'm Mette. I'm a 25-year-old Norwegian female. I'm living in Oslo, but originally I'm from a small town … located somewere near the Arctic circle.
I'm working in a company that provides telecommunications solutions (I'm in 'a man's world'). Search, analysis, development … I really like my job! Yes, I admit I don't think so when the alarm clock's ringing at 7 a.m. and I'm looking for it to turn it off : ))
The oficial company language is English, but my colleagues are Norwegian and Belgian guys. And I noticed recently that my English started narrowing so all I said was 'it's done, it's updated, it works fine now' and other job-specific terms. So your website is a ray of light! I feel more confident now with my English. Thank you a lot!
I like hanging with my friends, attending foto exhibitions (the last one was Anton Corbin), going to a movie. A bit of sport activity: swimming, pilates. I'm also learning French (as I lived in Belgium for 1 year and my Belgian friends test my French from time to time). And like I said, I love my work, but I'll probably try and find a job in the UK or France in the future, so my languages need to be good.

**11** Write your self-description for the ESL website. Remember the first tip and don't write more than 200 words!

# Interview Communication and technology



**1 Before you watch, think about how often you ...**

a use email.
b use mobile phones.
c use online chat services.
d use social networking sites.
e put your videos or pictures online.
f watch TV.

**2 Watch the video. Who talks about the activities in Exercise 1, Alan or Aurora?**

a ____________
b ____________
c ____________
d ____________
e ____________
f ____________

Alan

Aurora

**3 Are these sentences about Alan true or false? Watch again (0:11–1:08) to check.**

1 Alan works as a pilot. TRUE / FALSE
2 He thinks technological advances have both a good and a bad side. TRUE / FALSE
3 He likes the fact that with email, we can get and give immediate answers. TRUE / FALSE
4 He is worried because, as an older person, he can't keep up with the pressure of technological communications. TRUE / FALSE

**4 Cross out the things Aurora does *not* say. Watch again (1:12–2:07) to check.**

1 She posts videos / pictures / messages on the social networking site.
2 She likes the social network but sometimes it takes too much of her time / she wastes a lot of time.
3 She is a PhD student / needs the Internet for her studies / needs to focus on her studies.
4 Her friends are afraid that their boss / their colleagues / a future employer will see the things they post.
5 She isn't worried because she isn't working at the moment / doesn't have anything to hide.

**5 Can you remember which verbs from the box were used in these extracts? Watch again to check.**

access communicate expect give let post provide require stay use

**Alan**

... a lot of the information which we can [1] ____________ and which we are asked to [2] ____________ is often of an instant nature ... People will [3] ____________ instant answers, or [4] ____________ instant answers and sometimes we can't [5] ____________ that.

**Aurora**

One of the things I do to [6] ____________ with my family and friends in Puerto Rico is that I [7] ____________ the computer, social networks to [8] ____________ in touch. I usually [9] ____________ videos and pictures and [10] ____________ them know what I'm doing at the moment.

**6 Alan and Aurora both mention a negative aspect of the forms of communication they generally find useful. Look back at the things you considered in Exercise 1. Do you think they have any negative aspects?**

## GLOSSARY

**aircraft** (noun): another word for (aero)plane or airplane
**beneficial** (adjective): helpful or useful
**hire** (verb): to give someone a job
**hide** (verb): to keep something secret

# 3 Success

**VOCABULARY**
Talking about a business idea

**1** Complete this advice for selling your business idea using the correct verbs.

## SELL YOUR BRIGHT IDEA!

Have you [1]**c** *ome* **up with** a bright idea? Maybe you've designed a product that's **easy to** [2]**u**__________ and [3]**l**__________ **fantastic**? Want to [4]**m**__________ **money out of it**?

We'll help you to [5]**p**__________ **your idea**, get it on the market and – who knows? – you could [6]**m**__________ **a living** selling your bright idea!

Contact Ben Adler at Product Solutions
b.adler@productsolutions.com

**VOCABULARY**
Hopes, dreams and ambitions

**2** Put the words in the correct order, and add the verb in the correct form (*to* + infinitive or *-ing*) to complete these people's hopes and ambitions.

1. always / I've / wanted *I've always wanted to have* (have) children.
2. is / my / ambition __________________ (start) my own business.
3. of / thinking / I'm __________________ (do) some voluntary work when I retire.
4. like / one / I'd / day __________________ (travel) around South America
5. some / I'd / love / at / absolutely / point __________________ (have) a big old house in the country.

**Over to you**
Record yourself using the DVD-ROM: talk about some of your hopes, dreams and ambitions.

**VOCABULARY**
Abilities

**3** Read the descriptions of these people and complete the expressions using the words below or a preposition.

able ability capable facility good (x2) sense

1 Frieda is strong in interpersonal intelligence. She **is** __________ **to** communicate well and empathise with other people. She also enjoys working in a team.
2 Ana Paula has a logical-mathematical intelligence. She **has a** __________ **with** numbers and **excels** __________ complex calculations.
3 Jean-Claude has strong visual-spatial intelligence. He **has a** __________ visual memory and __________ hand–eye coordination. He enjoys visualising things and **is** __________ **of** mentally manipulating them.
4 Miki has a high bodily-kinesthetic intelligence. He **is good** __________ physical movement and enjoys performing in front of an audience.

5 Jacqueline has high intrapersonal intelligence. She is quite an introverted person and **is capable** __________ understanding her real feelings and emotions. She prefers to work alone.

6 Wilf is strong in verbal-linguistic intelligence. He **has the** __________ **to** use words and memorise things easily, and enjoys the discussions and debates that are part of his job.

7 Cindy Mae has a high level of musical intelligence. She **has a good** __________ **of** rhythm. Although she is not a professional musician, she enjoys singing in her local choir. She is good at listening to the people she works with.

**4** **Can you match the people in Exercise 3 with the jobs they do?**

| | | | |
|---|---|---|---|
| 1 | Frieda | a | writer |
| 2 | Ana Paula | b | music therapist |
| 3 | Jean-Claude | c | dancer |
| 4 | Miki | d | nurse |
| 5 | Jacqueline | e | astro-physicist |
| 6 | Wilf | f | photographer |
| 7 | Cindy Mae | g | radio presenter |

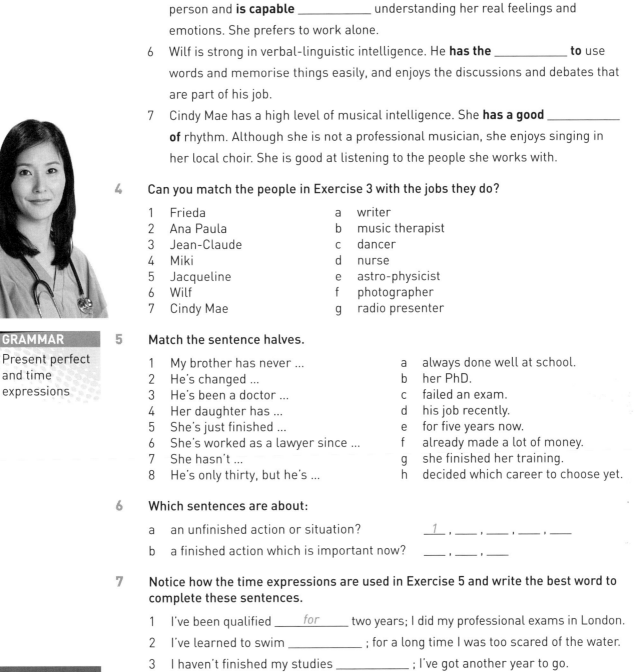

**GRAMMAR**
Present perfect and time expressions

**5** **Match the sentence halves.**

| | | | |
|---|---|---|---|
| 1 | My brother has never ... | a | always done well at school. |
| 2 | He's changed ... | b | her PhD. |
| 3 | He's been a doctor ... | c | failed an exam. |
| 4 | Her daughter has ... | d | his job recently. |
| 5 | She's just finished ... | e | for five years now. |
| 6 | She's worked as a lawyer since ... | f | already made a lot of money. |
| 7 | She hasn't ... | g | she finished her training. |
| 8 | He's only thirty, but he's ... | h | decided which career to choose yet. |

**6** **Which sentences are about:**

a an unfinished action or situation? _1_ , ___ , ___ , ___ , ___

b a finished action which is important now? ___ , ___ , ___

**7** **Notice how the time expressions are used in Exercise 5 and write the best word to complete these sentences.**

1 I've been qualified ___*for*___ two years; I did my professional exams in London.

2 I've learned to swim __________ ; for a long time I was too scared of the water.

3 I haven't finished my studies __________ ; I've got another year to go.

4 I've __________ preferred written exams to oral tests.

5 I've __________ had a couple of temporary jobs, but this is my first permanent one.

6 I've __________ played a musical instrument, but I enjoy singing.

7 I've __________ passed my driving test and I'm looking for a second-hand car.

8 I've wanted to be a vet __________ I was a child.

**Over to you**

**Choose four or five of the time expressions in Exercise 5 and use them to write sentences that are true about your life.**

**VOCABULARY**
Facts and feelings

**8** **Complete these extracts from a job interview using the words in the box. Sometimes more than one word is possible.**

concerned doubts excited information
optimistic passionate questions thoughts

1 Can you give me a bit more __________ about your career structure? [C]
2 I'd like to ask you some __________ about your professional background. [ ]
3 I'm very __________ about the possibilities the job would offer. [ ]
4 I'm interested to hear your __________ about working from home. [ ]
5 I've always been __________ about quality in customer care. [ ]
6 I have a few __________ about your ability to work under pressure. [ ]
7 One thing I'm __________ about is the financial aspect of the job; I don't have much experience in that area. [ ]
8 I feel very __________ about you working with the team. [ ]

**9** **Who says each sentence in Exercise 8? Write C (candidate) or I (interviewer).**

# MY English

**10** **Read what Andrey says.**

1 What is his problem?
2 How does he try to help himself?

In Russian there's no 'present perfect'. We just have a present tense and a past tense, so I find it very difficult to use the present perfect naturally in English. I say things like *I still didn't finish it* and *I'm here since two o'clock.* When I have time to think and remember the rules, I know I should say *I still haven't finished it* and *I've been here since two o'clock* but when I'm speaking to someone, I forget. I think people mostly understand me OK, but I feel quite dissatisfied with myself. I like music, and I try to remember words of songs to remind me how to say things correctly – I know *I still haven't found what I'm looking for* and *We've only just begun,* for example. It doesn't always help me at the right moment, but sometimes it works!

# YOUR English

**11** **Do you make similar mistakes with the present perfect? Can you change these sentences to use the present perfect correctly?**

1 I know him from 2006. *I've known him since 2006.*
2 How many years do you study English? __________
3 It's seven years that I live here. __________
4 He is become rich. __________
5 It's 8.20, and she still didn't come. __________

**12** **Andrey says he uses songs to help him remember the correct grammar. Do you know any of these 'present perfect' song titles?**

I've never been to me (Charlene)
I've just seen a face (The Beatles)
I've loved you for a thousand lifetimes (Michael Whalen)
I've just begun having my fun (Britney Spears)
I've waited so long (Foreigner)
Places I've never been (Mark Wills, country singer)

# EXPLORE Reading

Billy Bragg is an English singer, songwriter and guitarist

**13 Read the article quickly. Which success story does it describe?**

a How Billy Bragg learned to play the guitar.
b How Billy Bragg's son learned to play the guitar.
c How Billy Bragg's son learned to play Guitar Hero.

**14 Read the article again. Are these sentences true or false?**

| | | |
|---|---|---|
| 1 | Billy Bragg could play the guitar when he was 14. | TRUE / FALSE |
| 2 | Bill Wyman thinks Guitar Hero is a useful game. | TRUE / FALSE |
| 3 | Jack enjoyed playing Guitar Hero. | TRUE / FALSE |
| 4 | Jack was introduced to a real guitar by his father. | TRUE / FALSE |
| 5 | Guitar Hero helps you to learn basic hand movements for the guitar. | TRUE / FALSE |

# In defence of guitar heroes

**Billy Bragg**

When I was around 14, I became obsessed with the idea of being a guitar-player in a rock band. Having no musical ability, nor any instrument with which to make my dreams come true, I relied on my imagination, playing tracks on the stereo while playing along on my brother's tennis racket. In my mind, I was up there, performing in my favourite band.

Since the invention of Guitar Hero and similar computer games, it is no longer necessary to imagine what it would be like to play along with the Beatles – you can come together with them in the virtual world. Bill Wyman, former bass player in the Rolling Stones, has pointed out that music video games discourage kids from learning to play real instruments. My own experience suggests quite the opposite.

Last year, I bought Guitar Hero III for our 14-year-old son, Jack. Jack quickly mastered the process and entered an intense period of playing the game.

A few months later, while I was away on tour, a couple of his friends came around with a real electric guitar, wanting to plug it into one of my amplifiers. Playing Guitar Hero had taught them how to play along to a track. Now they wanted to see if they could apply that to the real thing. Jack's buddies taught him how to play along to his favourite songs using just his index finger on the bass string. He got it right away.

Guitar Hero had helped him over the first difficulty for guitar players – how to strum the strings with one hand while making chord shapes with the other. He never plays Guitar Hero now, preferring to rock out in the garage with his mates.

Despite my attempts at getting him to learn an instrument, it was Guitar Hero that taught him the basics of playing and built his confidence to the extent that he was able to make a recognisable sound the first time he plugged in.

So let's not complain about a game that encourages kids to become music fans and, in our son's case, gives them the basic skills needed to learn how to play guitar.

**15 Choose the best way to complete the sentence.**

Billy Bragg thinks Guitar Hero ...
a can encourage people to listen to music.
b can encourage people to play a musical instrument.
c can encourage people to listen to music and to play a musical instrument.

**16 Read this summary of the article and complete the phrases in bold with the correct preposition or adverb. You can find them in the article.**

When Billy Bragg was a teenager, he had to **rely** [1]___________ his imagination and 'play' a tennis racket like a guitar, but his son learned to **play** [2]___________ to songs with Guitar Hero. Later, when his friends **came** [3]___________ to his house and **plugged** an electric guitar [4]___________ an amplifier, he was able to **apply** his Guitar Hero skills [5]___________ a real instrument.

# Interview A proud moment

1 **Before you watch, think about a time when ...**

a you successfully learned a new sport or physical activity.
b you took part in a sports competition.

2 **Watch the video. Who talks about the things in Exercise 1, Saadia or Clare?**

a ________________
b ________________

Saadia

Clare

3 **Watch Saadia again (0:11–1:42) and circle the best way to complete the sentences.**

1 Saadia wanted to learn to ride a bike ...
  a because her friends had taken up cycling.
  b because she didn't enjoy hiking any more.
2 She ...
  a had never tried to ride a bike before.
  b had tried to ride a bike when she was a child.
3 She learned to ride a bike ...
  a on her own.
  b with her friends' help.
4 Saadia now cycles ...
  a every day.
  b every weekend.

4 **Saadia describes how she learned to ride a bike. Put these steps in a logical order. Watch again (0:11–1:42) to check.**

____ She learned to use the brakes to stop.

____ She learned to cycle on the road.

____ She learned to cycle alone.

____ She learned to pedal and manoeuvre the bike.

_1_ She learned to get her balance.

5 **Are these sentences about Clare true or false? Watch again (1:47–2:52) to check.**

| | | |
|---|---|---|
| 1 | Clare talks about a 100-metre race. | TRUE / FALSE |
| 2 | The race was outdoors. | TRUE / FALSE |
| 3 | Clare was worried about the angle of the race track. | TRUE / FALSE |
| 4 | She didn't win the race but was happy that she took part. | TRUE / FALSE |

6 **Both Saadia and Clare talk about their feelings. Who uses these expressions? Write S or C. Watch again to check.**

1 I was just really proud to be there. ☐
2 It was slightly daunting. ☐
3 I felt a bit left out. ☐
4 It was scary at first. ☐
5 ... which was frightening enough ☐
6 I thought no, I'm gonna get over that. ☐
7 Now, I'm a bit more adventurous. ☐
8 ... it was ... fairly daunting as well. ☐

7 **Look again at the experiences you thought about in Exercise 1. Can you remember how you felt?**

## GLOSSARY

**hike; go hiking** (verb): to go for a long walk in the hills or the countryside
**slope** (noun): a surface or piece of land that is high at one end and low at the other
**daunting** (adjective): making you feel slightly frightened or worried about your ability to achieve something
**pedal** (verb): to push the pedals of a bicycle round with your feet
**brake** (verb): to make a vehicle (here, a bicycle) stop or move more slowly, using its brake
**manoeuvre** (verb): to move with care or skill
**sprint** (verb): to run very fast for a short distance
**velodrome** (noun): a racing track for bicycles

4

# What happened?

**VOCABULARY**
Accidents and injuries

1 **Complete what the people A–C say about their accidents and injuries using the past tense of the verbs in the box.**

bang break (x2) cut drop fall slip ~~trip~~

A I *tripped* over a chair, ___________ over, and ___________ my face on the kitchen floor.

B I ___________ a plate on the floor and ___________ it , then I ___________ my finger on it when I picked it up.

C I ___________ on a wet floor and ___________ my leg.

**VOCABULARY**
Saying how something happened

2 **Put the words in the correct order to explain how the accidents happened.**

1 to / was / I / my / on / way ___________________________ the toilet and I didn't notice they'd washed the floor. ☐
2 the / I / in / middle / was / of ___________________________ cooking the dinner and I just didn't see it behind me. ☐
3 doing / the / I / washing up / was ___________________________ and it slipped out of my hand. ☐

3 **Match the explanations in Exercise 2 with the A–C in Exercise 1.**

4 **Cross out the expression which is *not* possible in these sentences.**

1 I was on my way home / to work / in the kitchen and tripped up.
2 I fell down the stairs / inside / over and hurt my leg.
3 I was in the middle of dinner / sleeping / washing up and cut myself on a knife.
4 I slipped and broke my face / a glass / my arm.
5 I tripped and banged my head / my knee / a plate.

## VOCABULARY
Natural events

**5 Complete the words for natural events.**

1 the n__________rn l__________

2 ts__________i

3 fo__________ fi__________

4 fl__________

5 v__________ic er__________

6 hu__________ne

7 ec__________

8 ea__________

**6 Read facts a–h and match them with events 1–8 in Exercise 5.**

a They're present all year round, but you can't see them in summer because it doesn't get dark enough. [1]
b They can start spontaneously in hot dry weather, but 90% are caused by human factors. [ ]
c They're getting more frequent and more serious as the level of the sea rises with global warming. [ ]
d The winds can reach 300 kilometres an hour. [ ]
e It's much easier to see a lunar one, as they can be seen wherever the moon is above the horizon. [ ]
f These can also occur underwater, sending steam and rocks above the surface of the sea. [ ]
g There are usually smaller 'aftershocks' after the main tremor, and these can continue for years. [ ]
h The water can be travelling at 800 kilometres an hour. [ ]

## GRAMMAR
Narrative verb forms

**7 Read Kath's description of the northern lights in Alaska and circle the correct verb form to complete the story.**

Kath, Canada

"It was a few years ago and we 1 had decided / were deciding to go away for the weekend. We 2 had driven / were driving back to our hotel when I 3 looked / was looking out of the car window and 4 saw / had seen green and pink waves of light in the sky. We 5 were stopping / stopped the car by the side of the road and 6 had watched / were watching the lights when a traffic cop 7 arrived / had arrived. When we told him why we 8 were stopping / had stopped, he 9 stayed / had stayed to watch them, too!"

**VOCABULARY**
Adverbs for telling stories

Hugh, England

**8** **Read Hugh's story about floods that happened in England and make it more interesting or dramatic by adding the adverbs in the box. There is usually more than one possible adverb you can use.**

amazingly immediately luckily obviously
quickly slowly suddenly unfortunately

We live quite near a river, so [1]__________ there is always a chance of flooding, but [2]__________ , the water has never got as far as our house. A couple of summers ago, we had a lot of rain and we watched the level of the river rising very [3]__________ , getting nearer and nearer. As we were watching it, the phone rang. It was the police, telling us to take all our furniture up to the first floor. We [4]__________ started to do this, but [5]__________ , we couldn't move everything, the bigger stuff. We just had to hope there wouldn't be too much damage to the ground floor. [6]__________ , the rain [7]__________ stopped and [8]__________ the water started to go down. We were so lucky.

**VOCABULARY**
Common verbs in stories

**9** **Read what Hugh says about after the water went down. Match the two halves of his sentences.**

After the water went down ...

| | | | |
|---|---|---|---|
| 1 | **I can't really remember** what ... | a | damage there had been. |
| 2 | **I realised** that ... | b | my first feelings were. |
| 3 | **I didn't know** how much ... | c | if our neighbours were OK. |
| 4 | I went to **find out** ... | d | we were safe. |

# TimeOut

## SOME JOKES ABOUT ACCIDENTS AND INJURIES

**10** **'Doctor, doctor!' jokes are popular in many English-speaking countries, but a book of jokes dating from the 3rd century contains an example of one, too, showing that the ancient Romans shared this sense of humour! Here are some 'Doctor, doctor!' jokes; do you think they are funny? Do you have 'Doctor, doctor!' jokes in your language?**

PATIENT Doctor, doctor! When I press my finger here on my arm, it hurts ... and here on my neck ... and here on my face. What do you think is wrong with me?
DOCTOR You've got a broken finger!

PATIENT Doctor, doctor! I've broken my arm in two places.
DOCTOR Well, don't go back there again!

PATIENT Doctor, doctor! My son has swallowed my pen! What should I do?
DOCTOR Use a pencil until I get there.

PATIENT Doctor, doctor! Every time I drink a cup of tea, I get a terrible pain in my eye. What do you think my problem is?
DOCTOR Try taking the spoon out of the cup!

**Over to you**

Think of a joke you know and tell it to someone in English.

# EXPLORE Writing

**11** **Read the first story from a website where people can share their experiences and put paragraphs A–D in the correct order.**

1 ___ 2 ___ 3 ___ 4 ___

http://www.experienceproject.com/

experienceproject

Groups | Experiences | Confessions | Answers | Blogs | People | More

## I found a new hobby!

**jojowrites**

A Unfortunately, the first day I was there was cold and wet so obviously not a good day for the beach! We were a bit disappointed, but decided to do a bit of sightseeing and got a bus to the nearest town.

B A few years ago, I went to visit a friend of mine who lives on the coast. It was summer time and we wanted to have a couple of days together on the beach, relaxing, chatting and swimming in the sea.

C I'd never been very interested in nature before, but now I'm out every weekend with the local wildlife protection group, walking, bird watching, tracking animals ... much more interesting than lying on a beach!

D When we got there, the only thing to visit was a funny little museum. It was the collection of a local wildlife enthusiast from the 19th century, and had hundreds of birds and animals from the area, which he'd preserved and displayed in glass cases. Weird but fascinating!

**luckyman7**

Cool! I had cold weather at the sea too last year. Hired a mountain bike the first day and headed for the hills. Fell in love with a beautiful lady there and never got to the beach ...

**autopilot**

My experience in Egypt earlier this year was the opposite – too hot to stay on the beach, so I headed UNDER the water. Did a diving course and my next holiday's going to be an underwater one.

**12** **Read the other two posts on the site. What do the three stories have in common?**

**13** **The first story is longer because it includes more detail. Which section(s) in the story ...**

1 include the writer's feelings about the experience in the story? _A_ , ___

2 explains the background to the story? ___

3 talks about the result of the experience? ___

4 describe details of the experience? ___ , ___

**14** **Write a similar short story for the website about how unexpected weather had a positive result. You can either expand one of the stories on the website, or write about an experience of your own. Remember to include the features in Exercise 13.**

# Interview A disastrous holiday 

**1** Before you watch, do this quiz to see how much you know about hurricanes. Tick (✓) the correct answers.

**1 A hurricane is a tropical cyclone.**
True ☐ False ☐

**2 In which ocean(s) can hurricanes occur?**
the Atlantic ☐ the Indian ☐ the Pacific ☐

**3 To be classified as a hurricane, there must be sustained winds of at least which speed?**
99 kph ☐ 109 kph ☐ 119 kph ☐

**4 Hurricanes can produce tornadoes and flooding. 'Storm surge' is flooding in:**
coastal areas ☐ inland areas ☐

**5 Which thing(s) would be useful to have in a hurricane emergency kit?**
food and water ☐ blankets ☐ clothes ☐
a mobile phone ☐ your personal documents ☐ a torch and batteries ☐

**6 The word hurricane comes from Huracan, a native Caribbean-Amerindian storm god.**
True ☐ False ☐

**2** Watch Matt talking about his experience of being in a hurricane and complete each sentence with one word.

1 Matt was on holiday in ________________ .
2 He was staying in a small ________________ .
3 He went out because he wanted to buy some ________________ .
4 He found a ________________ that was open.
5 He bought some cigarettes and ________________ .

Matt

**3** Match the words to describe what Matt saw. Watch again to check.

1 absolute
2 pylons
3 people
4 everywhere
5 collapsed

a taking shelter
b trees
c fallen down
d chaos
e totally locked up

**4** How does Matt describe his feelings about the experience? Complete his sentences using the words in the box. Watch again if you need to check.

anything chuffed crazy irritated nightmare starving worst

1 It was the ______________ holiday I've ever experienced.
2 It was just an absolute ______________ .
3 I've never seen or experienced ______________ like it.
4 I was getting really ______________ , ______________ , and I really needed some cigarettes.
5 That was another half an hour walk back and I was quite ______________ but everyone just thought I was ______________ when I came back.

**5** Matt knows he took a risk in going out in a hurricane. Would you know the correct way to stay safe in a hurricane situation? Find out by researching online, e.g. http://en.wikipedia.org

## GLOSSARY

**holed up** (adjective): staying inside (for safety)
**cabin fever** (noun): when you feel angry and bored because you have been inside for too long
**starving** (adjective, informal): very hungry
**pylon** (noun): a large metal structure that carries electric power lines above the ground
**take shelter** (verb): to go under a cover or inside a building to be protected from bad weather or danger
**chuffed** (adjective, informal): pleased or happy

# 5 A change of plan

**VOCABULARY**
*be supposed to, be meant to*

**1** **Look at Trinny's appointments and complete her part of the phone conversation using the phrases in the box.**

| to be going | supposed to | I'm meant | going to | meant to be |
|---|---|---|---|---|

Ellie! How nice to hear from you! ... When can we meet up? I really don't know. I've got a really busy week. I'm meant to be $^{1}$____________________ the doctor's tomorrow, but I'll have to cancel that – I've got a meeting with Jake. Then I'm having lunch with Diana on Wednesday. ... No, after that $^{2}$____________________ to be going to some talk about health and safety. ... No, sorry, on Thursday afternoon we're supposed $^{3}$____________________ to a meeting at the school. ... This evening? Well, I'm $^{4}$____________________ playing tennis – if I've got the energy. ... How about Friday afternoon? I'm $^{5}$____________________ complete my tax form by then, so after that I'll be more relaxed. ... Great, about three?

**GRAMMAR**
Future forms

**2** **Circle the correct verb forms to complete the conversation between Trinny and Ellie on Friday afternoon.**

**TRINNY** Hi! Come on in. Sit down and $^{1}$I'll make / I'm making some coffee.
**ELLIE** Great, thanks. So, have you had any ideas? What $^{2}$are we going to do / will we do?
**TRINNY** I don't know. Mark $^{3}$will pick / 's going to pick the kids up from school and take them swimming, so I'm free for a bit.
**ELLIE** Great! Why don't we go into town, then? The market's on today.
**TRINNY** Good idea. I need to get some food for the weekend, so $^{4}$I'm getting / I'll get something nice there.
**ELLIE** OK, great. $^{5}$I'm meeting / I'll meet some people for a drink at six o'clock, so we've got a couple of hours before that. Do you want to come along?
**TRINNY** No, thanks. I've got to cook for the family, then $^{6}$I'm going to chill out / I'm chilling out for the rest of the evening.

## Over to you

Write about some of your plans for the next week. Use *supposed to / meant to* and future forms.

**VOCABULARY**
*no chance, no way*

**3** **Complete the sentences using the words in the box.**

coincidence   surprise   use   way/chance

1 It's no __________ calling her now; the meeting's already started.
2 It was no __________ that we didn't get the job; our proposal was way too expensive.
3 There's no __________ we'll catch the nine o'clock train; we'll have to get the later one.
4 It's no __________ that we know each other; our daughters go to the same dance class.

**GRAMMAR**
Future in the past

**4** **Match the sentence halves to describe a weekend that went wrong.**

1 I was going with four other friends, ... ☐
2 We were supposed to leave early on Saturday, ... ☐
3 We were going to find somewhere to camp, ... ☐
4 We were going to spend the afternoon on the beach, ... ☐
5 We were going to go to a nice restaurant for dinner, ... ☐
6 We were supposed to get home the next afternoon, ... ☐

a but the car had a flat battery.
b but we had to spend all our money on a hotel.
c but then two of them got ill.
d but we got stuck in traffic till midnight.
e but all the sites were full.
f but it rained all afternoon.

**5** **Complete the sentences using the prompts in brackets.**

1 I *was meeting some friends* (meet / friends) for a drink, so I had to hurry.
2 She __________ (going / come) with us, but she had to go and see her mum.
3 I __________ (going / call) him, but I completely forgot.
4 I __________ (supposed / go / cinema) this evening, but I had to work late.
5 You __________ (supposed / be) here at 8.30; what happened?
6 We __________ (leave) on the early flight, so we packed our bags the evening before.
7 I __________ (going / go swimming) this morning, but I just didn't have time.

**VOCABULARY**
Catching up

**6** **Complete the conversation at the students' reunion using the words in the box.**

a long time   changed a bit   did you ever   didn't work out   I saw you
looking well   only yesterday   remember   you were going to

**ADELA** Hey, Cindy! Good to see you. You're [1] __________ .
**CINDY** You too. You haven't [2] __________ .
**ADELA** Well, I'm not sure about that – it's been such [3] __________ .
**CINDY** I know, but it seems like [4] __________ . By the way, [5] __________ get that motorbike you always talked about?
**ADELA** Certainly did – I've still got it, actually! And what about you? [6] __________ work in Africa, weren't you?
**CINDY** No, that [7] __________ . But I'm working for an aid and development agency, so it's the same field. How about you? The last time [8] __________ you were going to do an MBA.
**ADELA** Yeah, I did that, and now I'm working for a clothing company in Paris.
**CINDY** Ah, yes. I [9] __________ you were always interested in fashion.

**VOCABULARY**
Saying no politely

**7** **Put the words in the correct order to complete these sentences saying no. Add the correct punctuation.**

1 I'd / sorry / to / love ____________________ hear it, but I'm a bit busy right now.
2 great / but / that's / a / idea ____________________ I don't think it's that suitable for our target users.
3 I appreciate your offer of the position of office manager. I / however / feel / that ____________________ I am unable to accept this post.
4 don't / actually / I / think ____________________ I can answer your questions. Why don't you try Georges?
5 Yes, but I / I'm / afraid / can't ____________________ make it to the reunion.
6 we / unfortunately / are / not ____________________ able to help you at this moment in time.

**8** **Match sentences 1–6 in Exercise 7 with these sentences which come before them.**

a Thank you for your letter of 23 October. [3]
b Why don't we try advertising on local radio? [ ]
c Can you give me some information about the new course? [ ]
d We have received your request for funding. [ ]
e Did you get the invitation from the Old Students' Association? [ ]
f Can I tell you about my idea for the marketing event? [ ]

# MY English

**9** **Read what four people say about the use of English words in their languages. Which person (a–d) talks about ...**

1 an invented 'English' word? __________
2 an English word that's used in their language with a similar but confusing meaning? __________
3 an English word that's used with a completely different meaning and grammar? __________
4 a comfortable relationship between two languages? __________

**a** Last year I spent nine months at the University of Southampton in England. When I first arrived, I kept reading things like 'ask your tutor for advice', but I didn't know who my tutor was. I finally realised it meant the lecturer for my main course. The problem was that in Italian we use the word *tutor* but it means something like an assistant or adviser at university, not a teacher or professor.

**b** In German we call a mobile phone a *handy*. I knew the English name was different of course, but when I learned the English adjective *handy*, meaning useful or helpful, it was easy to remember as 'my handy is handy'!

**c** I was born in the US, but my parents came here from Mexico. When I'm with other Hispanic people, we tend to mix English and Spanish words quite freely. You hear things like 'voy para pick up mi hija' instead of 'I'm going to pick up my daughter'. It's even got a name – Spanglish!

**d** In France we use quite a few English words, like *weekend* or *email*. But there are some words that look like English, but are really just made up. When I did an English course in London, we were talking about celebrities (in French we call them *people*!) and I said someone had had a *relooking*. This is what we say in France, but none of the other students or the teacher understood it. I explained what I meant, and the teacher told me the 'real' English word was *makeover*.

## YOUR English

**10** **Do people think the use of English words in your language is a good thing? Make a list of English words that your language uses. Are they used in any of the ways described here?**

# EXPLORE Reading

**11** Look at this list of tips for planning a party. Are there any you don't think are very important?

https://www.wiki.questions/planning_parties

## How to plan a party

Article

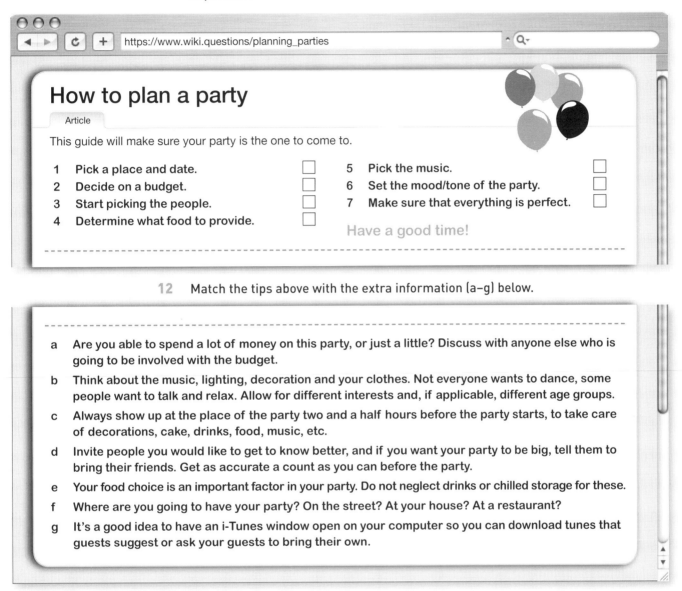

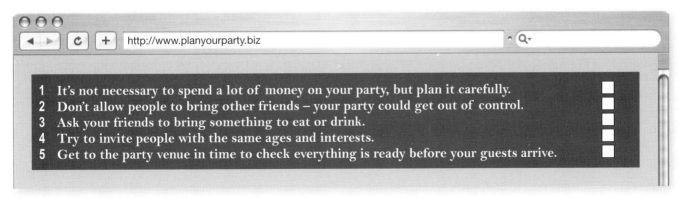

This guide will make sure your party is the one to come to.

1 Pick a place and date. ☐
2 Decide on a budget. ☐
3 Start picking the people. ☐
4 Determine what food to provide. ☐
5 Pick the music. ☐
6 Set the mood/tone of the party. ☐
7 Make sure that everything is perfect. ☐

Have a good time!

**12** Match the tips above with the extra information (a–g) below.

a Are you able to spend a lot of money on this party, or just a little? Discuss with anyone else who is going to be involved with the budget.
b Think about the music, lighting, decoration and your clothes. Not everyone wants to dance, some people want to talk and relax. Allow for different interests and, if applicable, different age groups.
c Always show up at the place of the party two and a half hours before the party starts, to take care of decorations, cake, drinks, food, music, etc.
d Invite people you would like to get to know better, and if you want your party to be big, tell them to bring their friends. Get as accurate a count as you can before the party.
e Your food choice is an important factor in your party. Do not neglect drinks or chilled storage for these.
f Where are you going to have your party? On the street? At your house? At a restaurant?
g It's a good idea to have an i-Tunes window open on your computer so you can download tunes that guests suggest or ask your guests to bring their own.

**13** Look at these tips from another website. Do they give the same advice as the first one, or different? Write S or D.

http://www.planyourparty.biz

1 It's not necessary to spend a lot of money on your party, but plan it carefully. ☐
2 Don't allow people to bring other friends – your party could get out of control. ☐
3 Ask your friends to bring something to eat or drink. ☐
4 Try to invite people with the same ages and interests. ☐
5 Get to the party venue in time to check everything is ready before your guests arrive. ☐

1 **Before you watch, think about these questions. Have you ever met up with a friend after many years? How did you get in touch with them?**

Fabiola

Leo

2 **Watch Fabiola and Leo talking about meeting up with an old friend again. Who ...**

1 arranged the meeting by email? ___________
2 got in touch through Facebook? ___________
3 had never met the friend before? ___________
4 met their friend again after several years? ___________

3 **Put these events in Fabiola's story in the order they happened. Watch again (0:11–1:58) to check.**

___ She went to university.
___ She invited her friend to visit her.
___ She started learning English.
___ She started work.
___ She looked at the old letters with her friend.
___ She started writing to her friend.
___ She found her friend on Facebook.

4 **Are these statements about Leo's story true or false? Watch again (2:02–3:11) to check.**

1 Leo didn't know his friend very well when they were at university. TRUE / FALSE
2 They enjoyed musical activities together. TRUE / FALSE
3 Leo's friend now lives and works in Japan. TRUE / FALSE
4 Leo was invited to his friend's wedding. TRUE / FALSE
5 His friend doesn't speak Japanese very well. TRUE / FALSE

5 **Who says these things about their friendship? Write F or L.**

1 We spent the most amazing weeks together. ☐
2 We kept in contact for about five years. ☐
3 I was really looking forward to meet(ing) her again. ☐
4 It was a very good chance to get to know people from a native country where they speak English. ☐
5 We've known each other for years and we know each other very well. ☐
6 We used to exchange lots of letters and also music.
7 I lost track of her. ☐
8 We were very close friends. ☐

6 **How easy do you find it to keep in touch with old friends? What different methods do you use?**

## GLOSSARY

**penfriend** (noun): someone who you write to regularly, but you have never met
**choir** /'kwaɪə/ (noun): a group of people who sing together
**be in the dark** (verb): to not know something that other people know about

# 6 Let me explain

**VOCABULARY**
Linking expressions

**1** Complete these money-saving tips with the correct linking expression.

after   if   in case   instead of   when   whenever

## SAVE MONEY …

### … around the home

1 Always turn off electrical equipment ___________ using it; leaving things on standby uses energy!

2 Use the washing machine at night, ___________ electricity is cheaper. And wash clothes in cold water ___________ using a hot water programme.

3 ___________ you have a printer at home, print on both sides of the paper you use.

4 Don't buy food you don't need; check your fridge before you go shopping ___________ you already have food that needs to be eaten.

5 Turn off the lights ___________ you leave a room to save electricity.

**VOCABULARY**
Multi-word verbs: managing money

**2** Circle the correct particle to complete the multi-word verbs in these tips.

### … and when you're out shopping

1 **Look out / over** for special offers in the supermarket, but don't buy things you won't use.

2 Work out your budget for food and try to **keep at / to** it.

3 If you **go out / over** your budget one week, try to stay under it the next week.

4 Try an experiment one week. See what is the minimum you can **survive on / for**. You'll probably be surprised!

5 Don't **give in / up** buying the things you like, but buy them less often. For instance, buy yourself some chocolate once a week instead of every day.

6 Put a small amount of money in an envelope every week to **save up / on** for occasional treats.

## VOCABULARY
Using equipment

Helga, Iceland

**3** **Complete Helga's computer story using the correct form of the verbs in the box.**

check click open plug press shut switch (x3) unplug

I had a really frustrating day yesterday. I needed to do some research, but I couldn't get online. I tried [1]__________ the computer off and on again, but that didn't help. I even [2]__________ everything down, [3]__________ all the different bits of equipment and [4]__________ it all into another socket, but that didn't solve the problem, either. I tried to [5]__________ the Internet connection, but after I'd [6]__________ on 'Control panel' and [7]__________ 'Network connections', I didn't understand the message it gave me! So I had to ring the helpline, and of course when I [8]__________ the number to speak to a technician, I had to wait for ages listening to really irritating music. I finally spoke to someone who was actually really helpful, and we found the problem. There's a little switch for the Internet connection on the side of my laptop, and it had somehow got [9]__________ off. I didn't even know it was there! I [10]__________ it on again and everything was fine. I felt so stupid – and I'd wasted a whole morning.

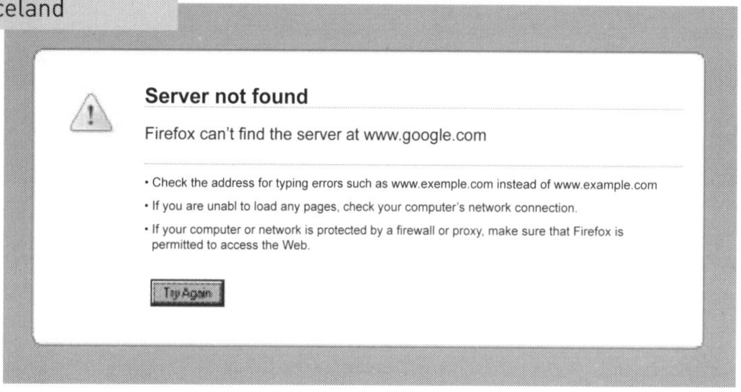
Server not found
Firefox can't find the server at www.google.com
• Check the address for typing errors such as www.exemple.com instead of www.example.com
• If you are unabl to load any pages, check your computer's network connection.
• If your computer or network is protected by a firewall or proxy, make sure that Firefox is permitted to access the Web.
Try Again

## GRAMMAR
Verb + *-ing*

**4** **Complete the conversation using the correct form of the verbs in the box.**

avoid can't face consider keep think try

**A** My car [1]__________ breaking down. I guess I'll have to [2]__________ about getting a new one.

**B** Oh dear. But do you really need one? I thought you cycled most of the time.

**A** Well, yes. I try to [3]__________ using it too much, but it's nice to have for weekend trips and things.

**B** Hmm. Have you [4]__________ car sharing? I think there's a scheme here for that.

**A** Yes, but a friend of mine [5]__________ using it and it was very expensive, and not really very convenient.

**B** Ah well, it looks like you *will* have to buy a new car, then.

**A** I know, but I [6]__________ selling my old one. I've had it for a long time, and it's like an old friend!

**VOCABULARY**
Giving reasons

5 Circle the correct expressions to complete this advice for new managers.

People are an organisation's most important resource, [1]so / because you need to get the best out of your staff.

Have an 'open door' policy [2]because of / so that employees know they can talk to you. Employee motivation is [3]because / due to many factors, including the opportunity to show initiative and participate in decisions; try to value everyone's contributions. Help individuals to develop professionally [4]so that / because this will help your organisation. [5]Since / Due to training is so important, this should be the last thing you reduce spending on.

[6]Because / So that negative feelings can spread quickly, you need to take action fast to solve any problems in your department. Many people suffer [7]because / because of unnecessary stress at work. Give people enough time, help and resources to do their job well.

And finally, make sure you act as a role model, [8]due to / as employees expect their bosses to set a positive example.

**Over to you**

**Which suggestions do you think are most useful? Are there any you disagree with? Write two more pieces of advice for managers.**

# TimeOut

6 **In the course book, you read about a German driver who crashed into a building because he followed his satellite navigation system too literally. Here are some more true 'sat nav' stories. Which one do you like best?**

A coach driver taking a group of nine-year-olds on a school trip to Hampton Palace, historic home of King Henry VIII, put the name of his destination into his sat nav and 60 children spent the whole day going round in circles after it directed him to a narrow street in north London with the name of Hampton Court. A journey that should have taken 90 minutes took eight hours, and eventually the children were taken back to the school. The only break in their journey was a stop for the toilet.

A gang of armed bank robbers were caught because their driver used his sat nav to check out locations for their raids. He added the addresses of 12 banks into his device's 'places of interest' while planning the robberies.

A group of workers on a Christmas outing to France were taken to the wrong country after a sat nav mistake sent them seven hours off course. The office outing was scheduled for the French city of Lille, but the group were diverted 160 km away to a village of the same name across the border in Belgium.

A Swedish couple wanting to go to the beautiful Mediterranean island of Capri drove to Carpi, an industrial town in northern Italy, because they misspelt the name in their car's GPS. The car's sat nav system had sent them 650 km off course. 'Capri is an island. They did not even wonder why they didn't cross any bridge, or take any boat,' said a tourism official in Carpi.

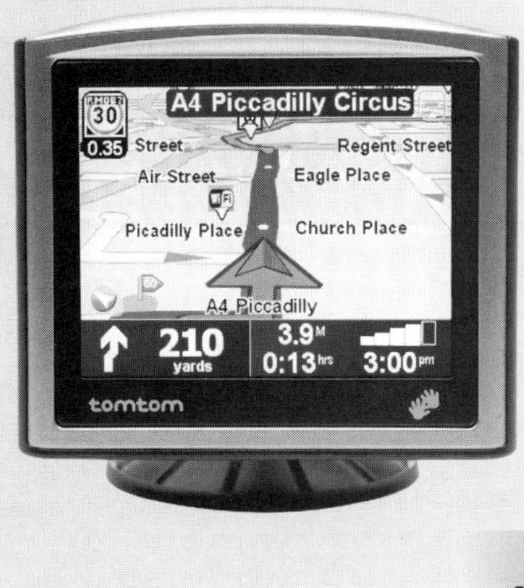


**Over to you**

See if you can find any other sat nav stories on the Internet.

# EXPLORE Writing

**7** **Read this note left by Simon for his friend, Ali, and answer the questions.**

1 How long is Simon going away for?
2 What is Ali going to do for him?

Hi Ali

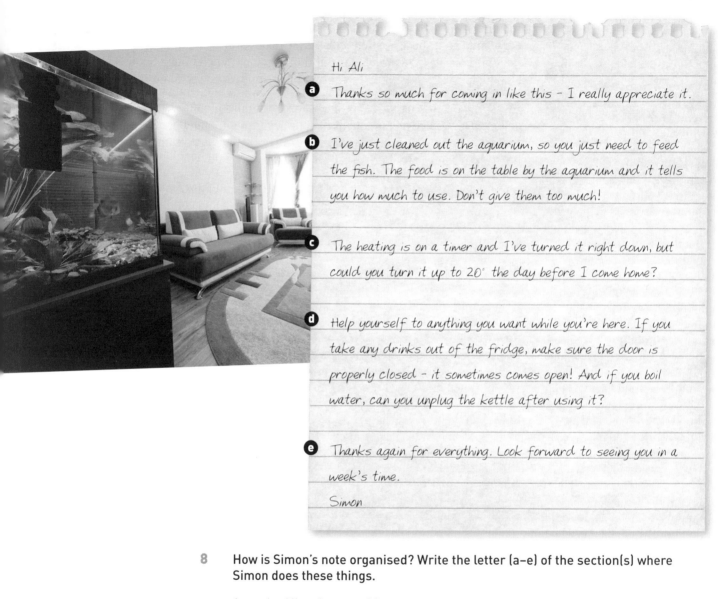

**a** Thanks so much for coming in like this – I really appreciate it.

**b** I've just cleaned out the aquarium, so you just need to feed the fish. The food is on the table by the aquarium and it tells you how much to use. Don't give them too much!

**c** The heating is on a timer and I've turned it right down, but could you turn it up to 20° the day before I come home?

**d** Help yourself to anything you want while you're here. If you take any drinks out of the fridge, make sure the door is properly closed – it sometimes comes open! And if you boil water, can you unplug the kettle after using it?

**e** Thanks again for everything. Look forward to seeing you in a week's time.

Simon

**8** **How is Simon's note organised? Write the letter (a–e) of the section(s) where Simon does these things.**

1 asks Ali to do something ____ , ____
2 thanks Ali ____ , ____
3 tells Ali what he can do ____
4 explains how to use equipment ____

**9** **Look at the note again and find ...**

1 three expressions used to say thank you
2 an expression that offers something
3 an expression that asks someone to check something is OK.

**10** **Imagine a friend or neighbour is coming to look after your house while you are away. Think about ...**

– things you want them to do (look after animals or plants, pick up post, ...)
– things they can do (use the garden, make drinks, ...)
– how to use any equipment (coffee maker, TV, ...).

**Write the note you will leave them. Don't forget to thank them!**

1 Before you watch the video, read this job description for a chef. How interesting / difficult would you find it to do this work?

**Job description – head chef**

- prepare and cook food according to the customers' requirements ☐
- plan, price and create a daily menu ☐
- arrange and garnish the food for serving ☐
- maintain cleanliness in the workplace ☐
- supervise health and safety in the workplace ☐
- be responsible for buying food ☐
- supervise delivery of supplies ☐
- supervise kitchen staff ☐
- carry out training of staff ☐
- prepare the specialities of the restaurant ☐

2 Watch the whole documentary and tick (✓) the things in the job description that Peter mentions.

3 Watch Part 1 of the documentary (0:06–2:27) and complete Peter's career profile.

**Training:** included 1 ___________ weeks work placement at the Reform 2 ___________, London.

**Work experience:** various jobs in restaurants and catering.

**Current position:** Chef manager for large 3 ___________, providing lunch for between 4 ___________ and 500 people daily in 5 ___________ restaurant and fine-dining restaurant.

**Main responsibilities:**

- 6 ___________ and safety
- staff training
- 7 ___________ purchasing
- hygiene of 8 ___________ and food

**Most enjoys:** working with 9 ___________ and food.

Peter

4 Peter describes a typical morning. Match his duties with the correct times. Watch again to check.

| | |
|---|---|
| 6.00 | Staff briefing |
| 6.30 | General check on kitchen and staff |
| 7.00 | Open restaurant |
| 8.45 | Briefing in restaurant (food, special client requirements, etc.) |
| 11.30 | Start serving lunch |
| 11.50 | Check food deliveries have arrived |
| 11.55 | Check kitchen is functioning |
| 12.00 | Staff arrive – check they know their duties |

5 Complete the multi-word verbs and other expressions Peter uses to talk about his day. Watch again to check.

carry check get go know make open should turn

1 My day starts between 6.00 and 6.15. The first order of the day is to ___________ **sure** the kitchen's functioning.
2 Then the rest of the team will ___________ **up**.
3 I'll make sure they're happy, **they** ___________ **what they're doing**.
4 I'll allow them to ___________ **on with it**.
5 Everyone will then ___________ **off** and ___________ **on with** their work.
6 Then I will ___________ **around** again that everything is **as it** ___________ **be**.
7 We'll be ready to ___________ **the doors** for 12 o'clock.

6 **Watch Part 2 (2:28–5:48). What is the best description of a Cambridge Burnt Cream?**

a It's a cold dessert made with eggs, sugar and cream, with a burnt sugar top.
b It's a dessert made with eggs, sugar and cream, served hot with a vanilla sauce.

7 **Match these descriptions with stages A–E below. Watch again to check.**

1 Pour mix into moulds and bake in oven. ☐
2 Heat cream gently. ☐
3 After chilling, sprinkle sugar on top and caramelise with gas gun. ☐
4 Add heated cream to egg mix. ☐
5 Whisk sugar and egg yolks together. ☐

## Ingredients

*free-range egg yolks*

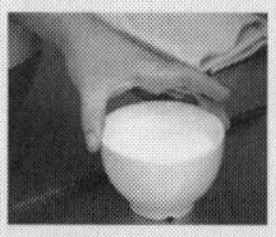
*whipping cream*

*caster sugar infused with a vanilla pod*

*sugar for caramelising*

## Stages

A
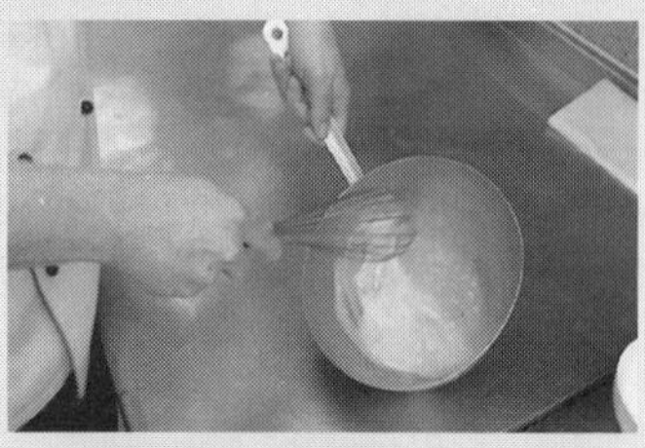

B

C

D

E
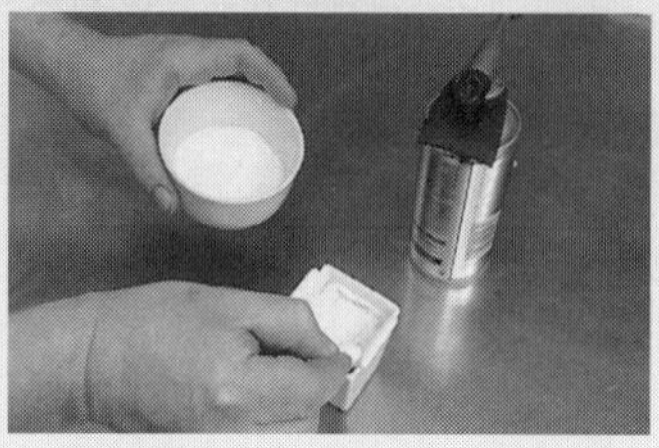

8 **Match these cooking verbs with their meanings. Watch again to check.**

| | |
|---|---|
| 1 whisk | a make something become hot or warm |
| 2 pour | b put in with something else |
| 3 heat (something) up | c present to be eaten |
| 4 boil | d mix something very quickly |
| 5 simmer | e put a small amount (e.g. of a liquid or powder) lightly on top of something |
| 6 add | f start to boil |
| 7 bake | g move a liquid from one container to another |
| 8 sprinkle | h cook in the oven |
| 9 serve | i (for a liquid) reach a high temperature and start to become a gas |

9 **Think of something you know how to prepare. Write a short description of what you need, and what the stages are.**

## GLOSSARY

**be hooked (on)** (verb): to like doing something very much, and want to do it all the time
**thoroughly** (adverb): very, or very much
**purchase** (verb, formal): to buy
**leave someone to their own devices** (verb): leave someone to do what they want to do
**briefing** (noun): a meeting to give people information and instructions
**infuse** (verb): to leave something like herbs or spices in food so it absorbs the flavour
**free-range eggs** (noun): eggs that come from chickens that live freely and eat naturally (not in **intensive** or **battery** farms)
**yolk** (noun): the yellow part in the middle of an egg
**curdle** (verb): If something like milk or beaten eggs curdles, it separates into solid and liquid parts.

# 7 Personal qualities

**VOCABULARY**
Personal qualities

**1** Complete what Sylvie says about the qualities needed in her work with these words.

an open mind   confidence   discipline   faith   initiative   talent

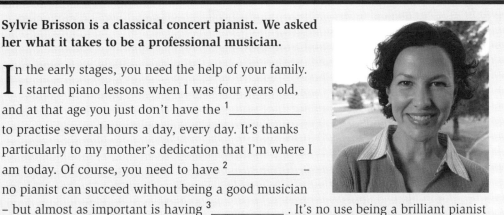

**Sylvie Brisson is a classical concert pianist. We asked her what it takes to be a professional musician.**

In the early stages, you need the help of your family. I started piano lessons when I was four years old, and at that age you just don't have the [1]__________ to practise several hours a day, every day. It's thanks particularly to my mother's dedication that I'm where I am today. Of course, you need to have [2]__________ – no pianist can succeed without being a good musician – but almost as important is having [3]__________ . It's no use being a brilliant pianist if you're too shy to play in public! When you get older it takes a lot of [4]__________ to go out and try to find work and make the professional contacts you need. You'll probably be offered different types of work, so you need to be quite flexible and have [5]__________ about things. And you'll have to face rejection along the way, so always have [6]__________ in yourself – believe that you can do it and you will!

**Over to you**

Which of these qualities do you need to have for the things you do? Write a short paragraph.

**VOCABULARY**
Matching people to jobs and activities

**2** Put the words in the correct order to complete what these people say about their jobs.

1. the / who / to / kind / be / you / person / need / of __________ isn't easily intimidated. People can be quite aggressive towards us.
2. is / my / job / that / something __________ you need both physical and mental fitness for. Often people fail because of their mental attitude.
3. that / the / job / kind / it's / of __________ needs a lot of initiative to solve new technical problems every day.
4. be / you / the / person / of / have / to / sort / that __________ absorbs information easily and can think quickly under pressure.
5. it's / of / the / sort / that / job __________ needs a lot of confidence to get out there in front of an audience.
6. to / be / who / need / you / someone __________ has infinite patience and attention to detail.

**3** Match these jobs with the correct people (1–6) in Exercise 2.

| | | | |
|---|---|---|---|
| a engineer | ☐ | d police officer | ☐ |
| b lawyer | ☐ | e tennis player | ☐ |
| c laboratory scientist | ☐ | f singer | ☐ |

**VOCABULARY**
Personality

**4 Match sentences 1–8 with sentences a–h to describe the people.**

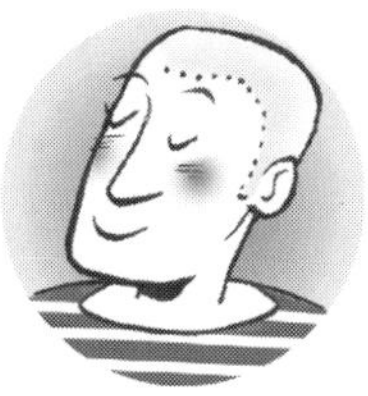

1 He's such a miserable character. [b]
2 He's a very calm person. [ ]
3 He's quite a difficult character. [ ]
4 He's such a charming guy. [ ]
5 He's a really nice guy. [ ]
6 He's a very interesting person. [ ]
7 He's an awful person. [ ]
8 He's a very bright guy. [ ]

a He's travelled a lot, and has lots of stories to tell.
b He never even says good morning when I see him.
c He's a great person to have around in a crisis.
d He says really unpleasant things about people, and expects you to agree with him.
e He's not at all easy to get on with, but I'm quite fond of him.
f He's only 25, but he's already running his own business.
g Everybody thinks he's wonderful when they first meet him!
h I've never heard him say anything nasty about anyone.

**GRAMMAR**
Comparing

**5 Read what Sylvie says about her relationship with her mother and cross out the expression in each group which has a different meaning.**

My mother has probably been the most important influence in my life so far, but we're quite different as people. She's [1]slightly / ~~far~~ / a bit more patient than me, and [2]much / far / marginally more tolerant of other people. On the other hand, I think I've got [3]a little / far / much more initiative than she has, maybe because she's always worked at home, looking after the house and our farm. I'm probably [4]just / nearly / almost as tough as she is mentally, although she's [5]a lot / slightly / much stronger physically. But we share the same sense of humour, and get on really well together – people say we're more like sisters than mother and daughter!

**Over to you**

**Choose two people you know well, and write three or four sentences to say how similar or different they are.**

**VOCABULARY**
Describing someone's influence

**6 Complete the expressions in the last part of the article about Sylvie Brisson with these words.**

made faith inspired interested to learn impression encouraged me

Apart from my mother, I've been very lucky to have had two teachers who have been fundamental influences in my life. The first was my very first piano teacher. She really **got me** [1]________________ **in** the piano and **made a huge** [2]________________ **on me** at a very early age. She **helped me** [3]________________ the basic techniques and develop an understanding of the instrument. Then, when I was 16, I started studying with my second inspirational teacher, Michael Bell. He [4]________________ **me much more confident** and [5]________________ **to** enter competitions and festivals even when I felt uncertain and unconfident about doing this. He **had enormous** [6]________________ **in me**, and it was this more than anything perhaps that [7]________________ **me to** make music my career.

**VOCABULARY** Roles and opinions

Nick, England

**7** Read what Nick says about his roles in life and complete the expressions in bold.

It's quite difficult to say what I [1]**def__________ myself as** first. I obviously [2]**see m__________ as** a husband and father as I have a lovely wife and three grown-up kids. But in my career, your family [3]**isn't reg__________ as** so important; your professional role [4]**i__________ seen as** the most important thing. I worked as a lawyer for many years, but was lucky to be able to retire when I was 50. I think that more and more in this country, retirement [5]**is perceived a__________** a positive and active time in a person's life. I'd **describe** [6]__________ __________ a hard-working person and in fact, I do quite a bit of voluntary work now I have the time, so I [7]**think __________ myself __________** a working pensioner!

# MY English

## A second language 'changes personality'

Psychologists have discovered that people take on different characteristics when they switch into another language. According to research, using different languages alters basic character traits such as extroversion and neuroticism.

**8** Read the newspaper extract above and the website posts (a–e) below. In which post does it say these things about speaking in a foreign language?

1 It's sometimes difficult to express your ideas, but this doesn't change your personality. ☐
2 You understand other cultures better, but you don't change. ☐
3 It's difficult to express your real personality. ☐
4 Thinking and saying things differently gives us a different personality. ☐
5 We should change the way we use our movements and our voice, too. ☐

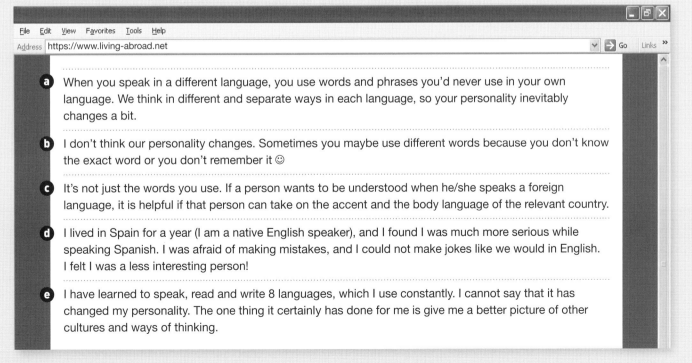

File Edit View Favorites Tools Help
Address https://www.living-abroad.net Go Links

**a** When you speak in a different language, you use words and phrases you'd never use in your own language. We think in different and separate ways in each language, so your personality inevitably changes a bit.

**b** I don't think our personality changes. Sometimes you maybe use different words because you don't know the exact word or you don't remember it ☺

**c** It's not just the words you use. If a person wants to be understood when he/she speaks a foreign language, it is helpful if that person can take on the accent and the body language of the relevant country.

**d** I lived in Spain for a year (I am a native English speaker), and I found I was much more serious while speaking Spanish. I was afraid of making mistakes, and I could not make jokes like we would in English. I felt I was a less interesting person!

**e** I have learned to speak, read and write 8 languages, which I use constantly. I cannot say that it has changed my personality. The one thing it certainly has done for me is give me a better picture of other cultures and ways of thinking.

# YOUR English

**9** What do you think? Write your own post for the website.

For more practice, go to Unit 7 of the Self-study DVD-ROM.

# EXPLOREReading

**10** **Read the introduction to a book about personality, *Please understand me II* by American psychologist, David Keirsey. Say whether the people (1–9) below believe …**

a people's behaviour depends on their inborn natural preferences
b people's behaviour depends on other factors.

| | | | | | | | | |
|---|---|---|---|---|---|---|---|---|
| 1 | Hippocrates | ☐ | 4 | Freud | ☐ | 7 | Myers | ☐ |
| 2 | Galen | ☐ | 5 | Watson | ☐ | 8 | Briggs | ☐ |
| 3 | Pavlov | ☐ | 6 | Jung | ☐ | 9 | the author of the book | ☐ |

The idea that people are born with very different innate temperaments or tendencies is very old. It was first proposed by Hippocrates around 370 BC and the Roman doctor, Galen, developed the idea around AD190. The idea continued in medicine, philosophy and literature up until the 19th century.

At the beginning of the 20th century, however, another idea was proposed – the idea that people are born without innate natural tendencies or preferences. Ivan Pavlov, a Russian scientist, said that behaviour was the product of a simple mechanical response to stimulation, and he claimed to have demonstrated this with his famous experiments on dogs. John Watson, the first American behaviourist, claimed he could form a child in any way that he wanted by 'conditioning' it to behave in a particular manner.

Alongside behaviourism, many investigators at the beginning of the 20th century also believed that people were fundamentally alike and shared the same basic motive for everything they do. Sigmund Freud claimed we are all driven from inside by instinct and although many of his colleagues and followers disagreed with him on other points, most of them kept the idea of a single underlying motivation for our actions.

Then in 1920, a Swiss doctor named Carl Jung disagreed fundamentally with Freud. In his book *Psychological Types*, he wrote that people are different in essential ways. He said that we have a natural, innate inclination to either 'extraversion' or 'introversion', combined with an inborn preference for one of what he called the 'four basic psychological functions' – 'thinking', 'feeling', 'sensation', 'intuition'.

In spite of Jung's work, for many years, the study of psychology was dominated by Freudian psychodynamics on the one hand, and Pavlovian conditioning on the other. Behaviour was explained as due to unconscious motives or to past conditioning, or to both.

Then, in the middle of the 20th century, an American woman called Isabel Myers and her mother, Kathryn Briggs, discovered Jung's book and, inspired by this, they designed a questionnaire to identify sixteen patterns of action and attitude. By the 1990s, over a million people were taking this questionnaire every year, and interest in personality types was restored in both America and Europe.

Perhaps people are not all the same, and their patterns of attitude and action are just as inborn as the shape of their body. Perhaps different people are intelligent or creative in different ways. Perhaps they communicate in different ways. Perhaps they want to learn different things at school. Perhaps they will be good at different sorts of work.

We can gain a lot by appreciating these fundamental differences between people, and lose a lot by ignoring them.

**11** **Read the article again and say whether these statements are true, false or not stated (NS) in the article.**

1 Medicine and philosophy shared many ideas for over a thousand years. TRUE / FALSE / NS
2 The majority of psychologists in the 20th century were followers of Freud's theories. TRUE / FALSE / NS
3 Pavlov and Freud had similar ideas. TRUE / FALSE / NS
4 Myers and Briggs' work helped to create new interest in the idea of personality types. TRUE / FALSE / NS
5 The Myers Briggs questionnaire is used a lot by psychologists. TRUE / FALSE / NS
6 The writer thinks we should understand and value people's differences. TRUE / FALSE / NS

**12** **Which do you think was the original title of this section of the book?**

a The influence of Sigmund Freud on 20th-century psychology
b A short history of psychology
c Temperament theory: Lost and found

## Unit 1

1 2 I used to 3 I'm not keen on 4 I hardly ever
2 2 don't watch 3 'm enjoying 4 use 5 prefer 6 've seen
3 2 Do you watch 3 Have you heard 4 Do you enjoy 5 Are you watching 6 Have you read
4 2 trust 3 inaccurate 4 scandal(s) 5 make up 6 fake
5 2 f 3 a 4 c 5 b 6 d
6 2 a really bad idea 3 a really good place 4 quite a good time 5 quite an easy way 6 quite a good idea
7 2 about 3 has 4 found 5 looks 6 say 7 well-known 8 based 9 shows 10 really
8 1 both 2 both 3 TV 4 book 5 both 6 both 7 TV 8 both 9 both 10 TV
9 1 Spanish 2 more
13 b
14 1 2007 2 David Attenborough 3 George Fenton 4 11 5 50 minutes 6 Planet Earth Diaries 7 Planet Earth: The Future 8 5
15 2 T 3 T 4 F

### INTERVIEW Different ways of life

2 1 S 2 M 3 S 4 M 5 M
3 1 F 2 T 3 F 4 T
4 1 c 2 b 3 e 4 a 5 d
5 1 relationship; family 2 business 3 anonymous; close 4 know 5 carry on; explain 6 helpful
6 1 from 2 to 3 to 4 to 5 for 6 from 7 about 8 behind 9 for

## Unit 2

1 1 reckon 2 I'd 3 say 4 no point 5 people 6 There's
2 1 to keep in touch 2 how many 3 surfing the Net 4 when 5 doing the same things 6 to leave your phone 7 to answer emails 8 what
3 2 use 3 have 4 like/enjoy 5 read 6 post
4 2 will be 3 I may not go 4 Her phone could be 5 Books won't disappear
5 1 be able to 2 will 3 when 4 will cause 5 you'll have to 6 it will be more difficult 7 it might actually help 8 you'll 9 might need to 10 it might be good
7 1 a 2 b 3 b 4 b 5 a 6 b
9 2 b 3 f 4 a 5 c 6 e
10 Suggested answers:
1 Yes – she gives a good picture of her work and free time.
2 Her home town, her family, her feelings about Oslo, what she did in Belgium, etc.
3 She adds some personal comments (e.g. about the alarm clock) and she uses some nice idiomatic expressions (*I'm in a man's world, a ray of light*).
4 The fact that English is her company's official language; her ambition to work in the UK.
5 line 3: somewere (should be *somewhere*); line 7: oficial (*official*); line 10: foto (*photo*)
6 Her work and her future ambitions.

### INTERVIEW Communication and technology

2 a Alan b Alan c Aurora d Aurora e Aurora f Alan
3 1 T 2 T 3 F 4 F
4 1 messages 2 she wastes a lot of time 3 needs the Internet for her studies 4 their colleagues 5 isn't working at the moment
5 1 access 2 provide 3 require 4 expect 5 give 6 communicate 7 use 8 stay 9 post 10 let

## Unit 3

1 2 use 3 looks 4 make 5 patent 6 make
2 2 My ambition is to start 3 I'm thinking of doing 4 One day I'd like to travel 5 At some point I'd absolutely love to have
3 1 able 2 facility; at 3 good; good; capable 4 at 5 of 6 ability 7 sense
4 1 d 2 e 3 f 4 c 5 a 6 g 7 b
5 1 c 2 d 3 e 4 a 5 b 6 g 7 h 8 f
6 a 3, 4, 6, 7 b 2, 5, 8
7 2 recently 3 yet 4 always 5 already 6 never 7 just 8 since
8 1 information 2 questions 3 excited/optimistic 4 thoughts 5 passionate/concerned 6 doubts/questions 7 concerned 8 optimistic/excited
9 2 I 3 C 4 I 5 C 6 I 7 C 8 I
10 1 His language doesn't have a tense like the present perfect, so he finds it difficult to use.
2 He remembers lines from songs which use the present perfect to help him with the grammar.
11 2 How many years have you studied English?
3 I've lived here for seven years.
4 He has become rich.
5 It's 8.20, and she still hasn't come.
13 b
14 1 F 2 F 3 T 4 F 5 T
15 c
16 1 on 2 along 3 around 4 into 5 to

### INTERVIEW A proud moment

2 a Saadia b Clare
3 1 a 2 b 3 b 4 a
4 2 She learned to use the brakes to stop.
3 She learned to pedal and manoeuvre the bike.
4 She learned to cycle on the road.
5 She learned to cycle alone.
5 1 F 2 F 3 T 4 T
6 1 C 2 S 3 S 4 S 5 C 6 S 7 S 8 C

## Unit 4

1 1 fell; banged 2 dropped; broke; cut 3 slipped; broke
2 1 I was on my way to 2 I was in the middle of 3 I was doing the washing up
3 1 C 2 A 3 B
4 1 in the kitchen 2 inside 3 sleeping 4 my face 5 a plate
5 1 the northern lights 2 tsunami 3 forest fire 4 flood 5 volcanic eruption 6 hurricane 7 eclipse 8 earthquake
6 b 3 c 4 d 6 e 7 f 5 g 8 h 2
7 1 had decided 2 were driving 3 looked 4 saw 5 stopped 6 were watching 7 arrived 8 had stopped 9 stayed
8 1 obviously/unfortunately 2 luckily/amazingly 3 quickly/slowly 4 immediately/quickly 5 obviously/unfortunately 6 Amazingly/Luckily 7 suddenly 8 slowly/quickly/immediately
9 1 b 2 d 3 a 4 c
11 1 B 2 A 3 D 4 C
12 They all describe a time when unexpected weather led to an interesting and positive result.
13 1 C 2 B 3 C 4 A, D

### INTERVIEW A disastrous holiday

1 1 True
2 All are possible, but the term 'hurricane' is only used in the North East Pacific and the North Atlantic Ocean.
3 119 kph
4 coastal areas, when the wind causes the sea to rise up above the land

5 All would be useful.
6 True

2 1 Cuba 2 apartment 3 cigarettes 4 supermarket 5 biscuits

3 1 d 2 c 3 a 4 e 5 b

4 1 worst 2 nightmare 3 anything 4 irritated; starving
5 chuffed; crazy

## Unit 5

1 1 going to 2 I'm meant 3 to be going 4 meant to be
5 supposed to

2 1 I'll make 2 are we going to do 3 's going to pick
4 I'll get 5 I'm meeting 6 I'm going to chill out

3 1 use 2 surprise 3 way/chance 4 coincidence

4 1 c 2 a 3 e 4 f 5 b 6 d

5 2 was going to come
3 was going to call
4 was supposed to go / be going to the cinema
5 were supposed to be
6 were leaving
7 was going to go swimming

6 1 looking well 2 changed a bit 3 a long time
4 only yesterday 5 did you ever 6 You were going to
7 didn't work out 8 I saw you 9 remember

7 1 Sorry, I'd love to 2 That's a great idea, but
3 However, I feel that 4 Actually, I don't think
5 I'm afraid I can't 6 Unfortunately, we are not

8 b 2 c 4 d 6 e 5 f 1

9 1 d 2 a 3 b 4 c

12 1 f 2 a 3 d 4 e 5 g 6 b 7 c

13 1 S 2 D 3 D 4 D 5 S

### INTERVIEW Reunions

2 1 Leo 2 Fabiola 3 Fabiola 4 Leo

3 3 She went to university.
6 She invited her friend to visit her.
1 She started learning English.
4 She started work.
7 She looked at the old letters with her friend.
2 She started writing to her friend.
5 She found her friend on Facebook.

4 1 F 2 T 3 T 4 F 5 F

5 1 F 2 F 3 L 4 F 5 L 6 F 7 F 8 L

## Unit 6

1 1 after 2 when; instead of 3 If 4 in case 5 whenever

2 1 out 2 to 3 over 4 on 5 up 6 up

3 1 switching 2 shut 3 unplugged 4 plugged 5 check
6 clicked 7 opened 8 pressed 9 switched 10 switched

4 1 keeps 2 think 3 avoid 4 considered 5 tried
6 can't face

5 1 so 2 so that 3 due to 4 because 5 Since
6 Because 7 because of 8 as

7 1 one week
2 feed his fish and turn on the heating before he comes home

8 1 b, c 2 a, e 3 d 4 d

9 1 Thanks so much / I really appreciate it / Thanks again (for everything)
2 Help yourself
3 make sure

### DOCUMENTARY The chef manager

2 prepare and cook food according to the customers' requirements
arrange and garnish the food for serving
maintain cleanliness in the workplace (hygiene)
supervise health and safety in the workplace
be responsible for buying food (food purchasing)
supervise delivery of supplies (check the early deliveries are in)
supervise kitchen staff
carry out training of staff
prepare the specialities of the restaurant (Cambridge Burnt Cream)

3 1 five 2 Club 3 company 4 400 5 staff 6 health
7 food 8 personnel 9 people

4 6.00 – Check kitchen is functioning
6.30 – Check food deliveries have arrived
7.00 – Staff arrive – check they know their duties
8.45 – Staff briefing
11.30 – General check on kitchen and staff
11.50 – Briefing in restaurant (food, special client requirements, etc.)
11.55 – Open restaurant
12.00 – Start serving lunch

5 1 make 2 turn 3 know 4 get 5 go; carry 6 check; should
7 open

6 a

7 1 D 2 B 3 E 4 C 5 A

8 1 d 2 g 3 a 4 i 5 f 6 b 7 h 8 e 9 c

## Unit 7

1 1 discipline 2 talent 3 confidence
4 initiative (*confidence* is also possible) 5 an open mind 6 faith

2 1 You need to be the kind of person who
2 My job is something that
3 It's the kind of job that
4 You have to be the sort of person that
5 It's the sort of job that
6 You need to be someone who

3 a 3 b 4 c 6 d 1 e 2 f 5

4 2 c 3 e 4 g 5 h 6 a 7 d 8 f

5 2 marginally 3 a little 4 just 5 slightly

6 1 interested 2 impression 3 to learn 4 made
5 encouraged me 6 faith 7 inspired

7 1 define 2 myself 3 regarded 4 is 5 as
6 myself as 7 of; as

8 1 b 2 e 3 d 4 a 5 c

10 1 a 2 a 3 b 4 b 5 b 6 a 7 a 8 a 9 a

11 1 T 2 NS 3 F 4 T 5 NS 6 T

12 c

### INTERVIEW Have you got what it takes?

2 1 V 2 R 3 V 4 R 5 V 6 V 7 V 8 V 9 R

3 1 F 2 T 3 F 4 T 5 T 6 F

4 1 skills; ability 2 stuff 3 faces 4 capability 5 need
6 ring 7 mainly 8 entails

## Unit 8

1 1 get 2 up 3 out 4 away 5 throw 6 give

2 1 working 2 instructions 3 come 4 play 5 do
6 condition 7 for

3 1 a nightmare journey 2 the wrong bus 3 got off 4 cancelled
5 got stuck 6 hitchhike 7 a lift 8 broke down

4 1 might/could 2 can't 3 might/could 4 must 5 must
6 might/could 7 can't 8 must

5 1 large brown leather 2 little pink plastic 3 big blue nylon
4 huge black metal 5 small multi-coloured cotton
6 medium-sized cream canvas

6 a 3 b 6 c 1 d 4 e 2 f 5

7 2 on the bottom d 3 inside c 4 on the top a
5 on the back b 6 on the outside / on the side f

9 1 a 2 b 3 d 4 c

10 1 g 2 e 3 a 4 c 5 b 6 h 7 f 8 d

11

| | Bicycle | Guitar | Cat | Sofa |
|---|---|---|---|---|
| A general description | | ✓ | | ✓ |
| Specific facts about the item, e.g. size | ✓ | | | ✓ |
| The condition of the item | ✓ | ✓ | | ✓ |
| Extras or accessories included | ✓ | ✓ | ✓ | |
| The reason the person is selling it | | ✓ | ✓ | ✓ |
| Who the item would be good for | | ✓ | ✓ | |

### INTERVIEW Nightmare journeys

2 Clare: b Andrés: a
3 1 h 2 f 3 e 4 a 5 g 6 b 7 d 8 c
4 1 The group that we were in weren't **particularly** good at map reading.
2 We decided to follow a river, not realising that it **really** made a difference which side of the river we were on.
3 So **eventually** at about 11 o'clock at night, we'd managed to get ourselves on top of a hill.
4 We thought we could see what looked like the rest of our group camping down below, so we started signalling SOS on our torches and **luckily** it was our group.
5 Everybody had eaten, they were **fast** asleep, we **still** had to pitch our tent and get up at five o'clock the next morning.
5 1 F 2 T 3 F 4 T 5 F 6 T 7 T 8 F
6 1 to 2 without; to 3 of 4 To; on; in 5 for

## Unit 9

1 1 power d 2 batteries c 3 pipe a 4 window b
2 1 handle 2 flat 3 pipe 4 burst 5 handle
3 1 I'll give it a try 2 What are we going to do 3 I'll have a go
4 What shall we do 5 We'll have to get
6 Well, we're going to have to
4 1 running 2 solve 3 brainstorming 4 listen 5 trust
6 look 7 come 8 develop 9 make
5 1 had 2 see 3 'll / will do 4 opened 5 feel 6 had
7 'll / will go 8 knew
6 1 How 2 mean 3 just 4 That 5 if 6 could 7 say
7 1 b 2 c 3 d 4 e 5 f (*d* is also possible) 6 a
8 b
10 b sentences
11 1 2 b
2 3 b
3 4 b (in sentence 3 b, *If you're ready* is an introductory phrase, but without the sense of apologising)
4 1 b (*maybe*); 4 b (*seems*)
5 1 b; 4 b
6 1 b (*slight*)
12 A **farmer** owed some money to a moneylender, but **the moneylender said he would marry the farmer's daughter** instead of **demanding** the debt. The girl **didn't like** the moneylender because he was **old and ugly**. The **girl and her father were** not happy, so **the moneylender** suggested they should use a random game to decide what would happen. **He** put two stones in a bag and said that if the girl picked a white stone, she **wouldn't have to** marry the moneylender. But he cheated and put only black stones in the bag. The girl saw this and didn't know what to do.
13 1 She can only pick a black stone, so she will have to marry the moneylender.
2 She won't have to marry the moneylender, but her father will have to go to prison.
14 2

### DOCUMENTARY The hairdressing entrepreneurs

1 1 more 2 more
3 2
4 1 F 2 T 3 T 4 F 5 T 6 T
5 1 advanced; traditional 2 comfortable 3 standards; invest
4 suspend 5 open more salons
6 1 i 2 h 3 e 4 g 5 c 6 a 7 f 8 d 9 b
7 1 find; earn 2 come up with 3 enjoyed 4 improve
5 look after 6 makes 7 pass on 8 stand out
8 1 company 2 marketing 3 work
9 company; work
10 1 apprenticeship 2 qualified 3 business 4 quality control
5 market 6 recession 7 expand 8 train

## Unit 10

1 1 reminds 2 recognise 3 can't 4 remember
5 noticed 6 I've 7 can remember 8 Looking
2 1 meeting 2 to charge 3 stayed 4 to send
5 to access 6 had 7 doing 8 was
3 a 3 b 2 c 4 d 1
4 1 page 2 magazine 3 car 4 colour 5 jacket
5 1 've / have been waiting
2 've / have written; haven't had
3 've / have been staying; 've / have charged
4 've / have been trying
5 've / have been repairing
6 've / have been waiting
7 has provided
8 've / have been trying
6 1 been 2 just 3 be 4 bit 5 to 6 really
7 **Across**
2 flat 4 flooded 5 power 8 scratched 10 wrong
11 dented
**Down**
1 faded 3 come 6 working 7 leaking 9 cracked 12 torn
8 1 a, b 2 a, b 3 b, c 4 b, c 5 b, c
9 1 e 2 b 3 a 4 f 5 c 6 d 7 g
10 1 receptionist 2 food 3 value 4 service 5 location

### INTERVIEW Witnessing a crime

2 a Aurora b Carlos
3 1 morning 2 jogging 3 handbag 4 stop him 5 five
6 three 7 month 8 South America
4 1 F 2 T 3 F 4 T 5 F
5 1 relieved, proud 2 relieved, grateful 3 embarrassed, sorry
4 angry 5 embarrassed, guilty
6 1 c 2 e 3 a 4 d 5 b 6 f
7 1 run away 2 run after 3 took ... back 4 growing up
5 running around 6 came back

## Unit 11

1 2 c 3 g 4 a 5 b 6 e 7 d
2 1 I said him 2 he say 3 I like 4 he saying 5 I goes
3 1 asked 2 explained 3 say 4 asked 5 say
6 agreed 7 said 8 say 9 promised
4 1 spoken 2 said 3 told 4 heard 5 heard
6 said 7 hear 8 heard 9 spoke
5 1 brought up 2 forced 3 encouraged 4 unacceptable
5 expected 6 happy 7 acceptable
6 1 F 2 T
8 Suggested answers:
1 Lovely day today, isn't it? / What awful weather!
2 Did you have a good journey? / It took me hours to get here this morning!
3 This is the first time I've sat down today!
4 Did you see that story about ... ?
10 1 HW 2 JB 3 HW, JB 4 MK, JB 5 MK, JB 6 MK
11 1 b 2 a 3 a

### INTERVIEW Family customs

2 b
3 d
4 1 F 2 T 3 T 4 F 5 T
5 1 England 2 50 3 boys 4 girl 5 50
6 1 throughout 2 around 3 towards 4 for 5 always
6 Due 7 since 8 on
7 1 N 2 D 3 I 4 D 5 N 6 I 7 N 8 N

## Unit 12

1 1 going to 2 talk about 3 start with 4 all 5 move on
6 Are 7 there 8 finally 9 Any 10 further
2 1 mind 2 tell (*give* is also possible) 3 ask 4 think
5 Would 6 do 7 Could (*Can* is also possible)
3 a 2, 4, 7 b 3, 6 c 5 d 1
4 1 a Could I ask you / Could you tell me which bank you have an account with?
b Could I ask you / Could you tell me if you are satisfied with the service?
2 a Could I ask you / Could you tell me how often you go to your nearest supermarket?
b Could I ask you / Could you tell me if you are happy with the range of products offered?
3 a Could I ask you / Could you tell me if you ever go to the cinema?
b Could I ask you / Could you tell me how many films you see in a year?
4 a Could I ask you / Could you tell me if you use the public transport in this area?
b Could I ask you / Could you tell me how efficient the service is?
5 a Could I ask you / Could you tell me how many cafés or restaurants there are in your area?
b Could I ask you / Could you tell me if you eat out more for lunch, or dinner?
5 2 That's **a** good question.
3 **it** depends
4 All I **can** say is
5 That's **an** important point.
6 I'll find **out** for you.
7 I'll get **back** to you
6 1 f 2 g 3 a 4 d 5 e 6 b 7 h 8 c
7 Slide b is better. The writing is bigger and clearer; there's not too much information for people to read; it only contains the main points, so it's more immediate and easier to understand. It also contains an example of a word square, so the audience can see what is meant.
8 1 contain the main points of the talk
2 use note form, abbreviations and bullet points
3 have a lot of white space around the text
4 not use distracting special effects
9 First modern crossword **1913, *New York World***
Became popular **in USA**
**First crosswords in UK** 1920s

### INTERVIEW Making presentations

2 1 A 2 E 3 E 4 A 5 E 6 E 7 A
3 1 F 2 F 3 T 4 F
4 1 trains volunteers 2 community groups 3 isn't 4 uses
5 1 nervous; in front of 2 auditorium 3 list
4 rehearse; whoever 5 channel; open your mouth
6 hard-and-fast 7 stuff; bring in

## Unit 13

1 1 fired 2 took over 3 built up 4 resigned
5 taken over 6 bankrupt 7 set up 8 run
2 1 shouldn't have refused
2 should have accepted; could have earned
3 could have joined; should have gone
3 1 risked 2 by 3 save 4 thank 5 rescuing
6 left 7 thinking 8 helps 9 favours
4 1 'd / would have helped; 'd / had known
2 hadn't / had not been; wouldn't / would not have started
3 'd / had come; 'd / would have asked
4 'd / would have finished; hadn't / had not crashed
5 'd / had stayed; would have grown up
6 wouldn't / would not have bought; 'd / had seen
7 wouldn't / would not have told; 'd / had known
8 hadn't / had not eaten; wouldn't / would not have had
5 1 told 2 known 3 should 4 better 5 asked
6 1 you're not allowed to 2 let you 3 make you
4 you're supposed to
7 face to face
12 1 G 2 D 3 B 4 F 5 K 6 I
13 1 K 2 H 3 E 4 D, M 5 C

### INTERVIEW We all make mistakes

2 1 T 2 B 3 N
3 1 F 2 T 3 F 4 F 5 T 6 T
4 1 He volunteered to work on a fundraising campaign.
2 He set up equipment for a conference.
3 He worked as a guard on a door.
4 He refused to allow Bill Clinton to go through the door.
5 He made some bodyguards angry.
6 He allowed Bill Clinton to go through the door.
5 1 not very good; confused 2 wrong 3 without 4 gone wrong
5 upset 6 responsible; make sure 7 told; different
8 not realised

## Unit 14

1 1 Firefighters 2 scene 3 residents 4 evacuated
5 motorists 6 arrested 7 involved 8 injured 9 offences
10 law 11 Police 12 oppose
2 1 What's good is that 2 The thing that makes me angry
3 The thing that worries me is 4 What's funny is
5 What depresses me is that 6 What's important is that
3 a 2 b 5 c 3 d 6 e 1 f 4
4 1 broke out 2 were called 3 was hurt
4 was found 5 is thought 6 called
7 have announced 8 said 9 will be given
5 1 was injured 2 has been donated 3 be used
4 is believed 5 are being made
6 1 read 2 about 3 who 4 heard 5 saying 6 hear
7 talking 8 Apparently 9 said
7 1 looks 2 's / has got 3 convinced 4 go 5 interesting
6 want 7 know 8 understand 9 makes
8 1 a 2 c 3 b 4 a 5 c 6 c
9 1 Don't blame the system for winter chaos. Stay at home.
2 23 December 3 Simon Jenkins 4 b
10 1 c 2 a 3 b
11 1 b 2 c 3 a

### DOCUMENTARY The runner

1 1 42 2 490 3 1896 4 3 5 1921 6 500 7 tens 8 15 9 2
2 why he likes running
having the right equipment
other types of exercise
involving your family
3 1 running 2 shoes 3 12; 16 4 swimming 5 Warming up
6 Stretch 7 Carbohydrates; energy 8 Fat(s) 9 fluid(s)
4 1 c 2 d 3 a 4 e 5 b
5 1 best 2 reached 3 worst 4 high
6 1 complete overview 2 good advice 3 prevent injury
4 training 5 different sessions 6 build up
7 diet and nutrition 8 intake

# Interview Have you got what it takes?

1 Before you watch, think about these questions. Do you think you would be a good teacher or sales executive? What skills and qualities do you think are needed for these jobs?

2 Watch Raquel (a teacher) and Valerie (a sales executive) talking about their jobs. Who talks about these skills and qualities? Write R or V.

1 being determined ☐
2 being good at explaining things ☐
3 having patience ☐
4 being able to simplify things ☐
5 being persuasive ☐
6 being good at smiling ☐
7 not being scared ☐
8 having a positive attitude ☐
9 being able to pass on knowledge ☐

Raquel

Valerie

3 Are these statements true or false? Watch again to check.

1 Raquel believes it's not necessary for a teacher to be clever. TRUE / FALSE
2 She says she can see when her students understand something she's explaining. TRUE / FALSE
3 Her colleagues have told her she's a good teacher. TRUE / FALSE
4 Valerie spends a lot of time calling customers. TRUE / FALSE
5 She believes you can hear when someone is smiling. TRUE / FALSE
6 She thinks it's important to close a deal in a day. TRUE / FALSE

4 Complete the extracts using the words in the box. Watch again to check.

ability capability entails faces mainly need ring skills stuff

**Raquel**

1 The ___________ necessary to be a good teacher in my opinion are the ___________ to pass on knowledge ...
2 You not only have to be very clever and to know a lot of ___________ ...
3 I think I have those skills because I've seen it in their ___________ when I teach.
4 I have the skill, the ___________ of explaining things, simplifying.

**Valerie**

5 As a sales executive, you ___________ to be very persuasive ...
6 ... not scared to ___________ people up.
7 My job is ___________ on the phone.
8 The job ___________ a lot of chasing.

5 Which job would you prefer to have?

## GLOSSARY

**get it** (verb, informal): to understand something
**chase** (verb): to try hard to get or catch something (in this case, probably a new customer or a new contract)
**close a deal** (verb): to be successful in getting an agreement with a customer
**entail** (verb): to involve something

# 8 Lost and found

**VOCABULARY**
Multi-word verbs: tidying and cleaning

**1** Complete the multi-word verbs in the advertisement.

## FREE SHOP

**Do you have stuff you want to [1]__________ rid of?**

Have you tidied [2]__________ your house or garage recently? Are you cleaning [3]__________ your flat? Is there no more space in your home to put [4]__________ your things?

**Don't [5]__________ away your clutter!**

If you don't want it, [6]__________ it away! Bring it to us and we'll find a new owner for it.

**VOCABULARY**
Describing products

Margot, Netherlands

**2** Margot works in her local free shop. Circle the correct words to complete what she says.

"I've just started working here three afternoons a week and I'm loving it. It's amazing what good stuff people bring in. Most of the electrical things are in good [1]working / condition order, and often the [2]directions / instructions are included or they [3]come / go with extra accessories, too. If someone brings in something that can [4]play / do up sometimes, they're very honest about that and we mention it on the label we attach to it.
Then a lot of people bring in really nice clothes and bags. Sometimes they could [5]get / do with a clean or a small repair, but mainly they're in good [6]condition / conditioning. The whole concept is ideal [7]with / for people who want to reduce the amount of stuff we throw away – or just people who like to find a bargain!"

**VOCABULARY**
Travel situations

Bryn, Wales

**3** Complete what Bryn says using the words in the box. Put the verbs in the correct form.

a lift a nightmare journey break down cancelled get off get stuck hitchhike the wrong bus

"I'd bought a second-hand motorbike on the Internet from someone who only lived 40 km away from me. I decided to get the bus there to pick it up, but I had [1]__________. First, I got on [2]__________, or rather the right bus, but going the wrong way. When I realised, I [3]__________ when we got to the train station in the next town. Unfortunately, all the trains had been [4]__________ that day because of engineering work on the line, so I had to wait another hour to get the bus back to where I started from. It was rush hour by then and we [5]__________ in a traffic jam, and by the time I got back, there weren't any more buses going to the other town that day. So I decided to try and [6]__________. I was surprised when a car soon stopped and a really nice guy gave me [7]__________. He said he'd drive me all the way, but – can you believe this? – his car [8]__________ on the motorway after about 10 km. It just convinced me how much I really needed that motorbike!"

**GRAMMAR**
Modals of deduction and speculation

**4** Margot is talking to one of her colleagues in the free shop about some things that have been brought in to the shop. Complete what they say with *must*, *might/could* or *can't*.

**MARGOT** Oh, look at this strange thing. What is it?
**CLARA** No idea! It [1] ____________ be some sort of kid's toy.
**MARGOT** No, it [2] ____________ be that. It'd be too dangerous with all those metal bits on. Maybe it's something you use in the kitchen.
**CLARA** Yes, it [3] ____________ be something like that. Oh yes, look. There's a food processor here – it [4] ____________ be an accessory for that.
**MARGOT** Wow! Look at this jacket. That's really cool.
**CLARA** Yeah, that [5] ____________ be pretty old – look, the buttons are made of bone, not plastic. I think it [6] ____________ be from the 1920s or 30s.
**MARGOT** No, it [7] ____________ be that old. I'd say 1950s, perhaps.
**CLARA** Maybe you're right. I'm sure it [8] ____________ be quite valuable, though, don't you think?

**VOCABULARY**
Describing objects

**5** Put the adjectives in the correct order.

1 It's a large / leather / brown ________________________ one.
2 It's a pink / plastic / little ________________________ one.
3 It's a big / nylon / blue ________________________ one.
4 It's a metal / black / huge ________________________ one.
5 It's a multi-coloured / small / cotton ________________________ one.
6 It's a canvas / cream / medium-sized ________________________ one.

**6** Match pictures a–f with descriptions 1–6 in Exercise 5.

a

b
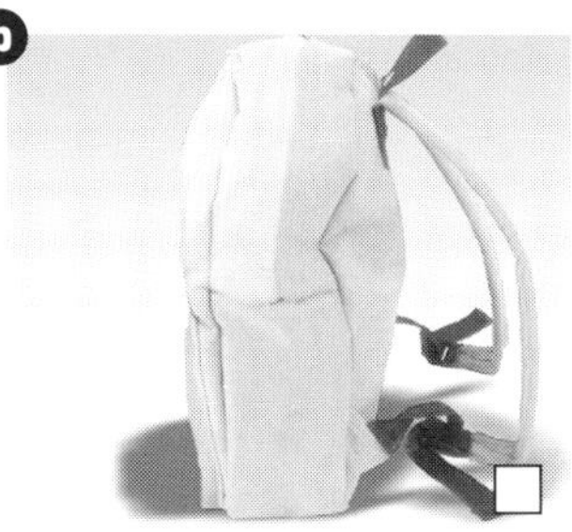
c
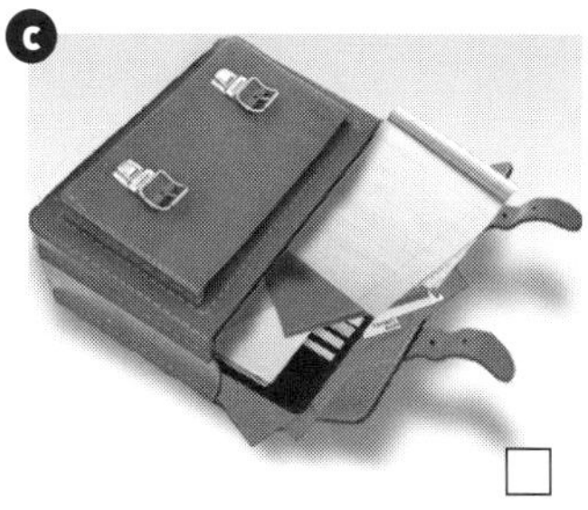
d
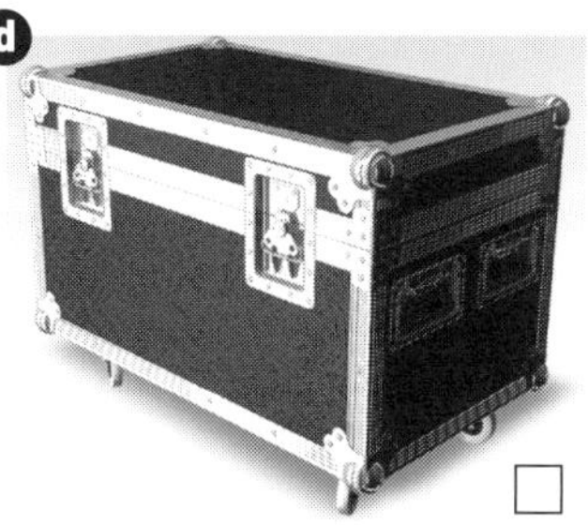
e

f

**7** Match sentences 1–6 with bags a–f and complete the descriptions with a suitable expression.

1 It's got a picture of a cat ___*on the front*___ . [e]
2 It has wheels ________________________ . [ ]
3 It's got some books and papers ________________________ . [ ]
4 There's a zip ________________________ . [ ]
5 It's got straps ________________________ . [ ]
6 It has a pocket ________________________ . [ ]

8 Do this quiz from a writer's blog.

http://www.happiness-project.com/happiness_project/2006/07/this_wednesday__2.html

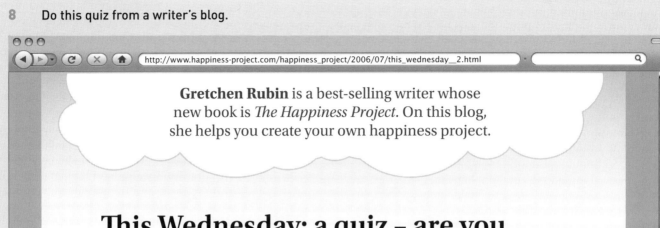

**Gretchen Rubin** is a best-selling writer whose new book is *The Happiness Project*. On this blog, she helps you create your own happiness project.

# This Wednesday: a quiz – are you organised or disorganised?

Most people understand that it's really annoying to be disorganised. Disorganised people spend a lot of time looking for their keys; they have to get a copy of their birth certificate; they have a dozen hammers, because it's always easier to buy a new one than to find one in the house.

Often, however, people don't realise how disorganised they are. Are you? Take this quiz.

You should know exactly where to find these possessions if you have them (and you should have them):

stamps
your passport and, if you're married, your partner's passport
a bottle opener
plasters for small cuts
a safety pin
a torch
an alarm clock
paperclips
your phone charger
an extra set of house keys
your doctor's phone number
your tax statements from 2003
a pair of gloves
AA batteries

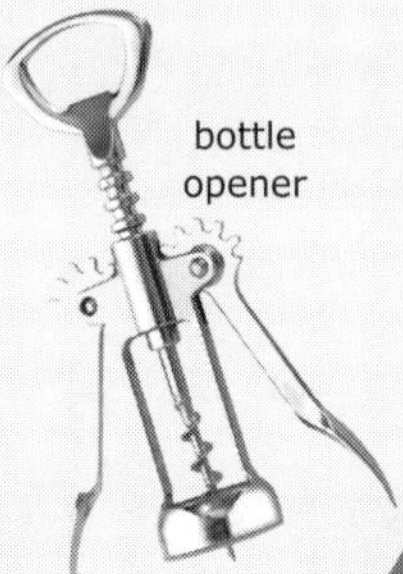

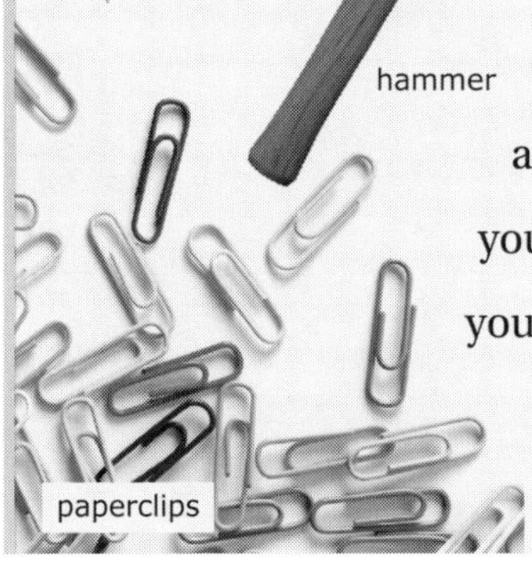


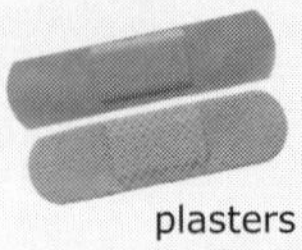


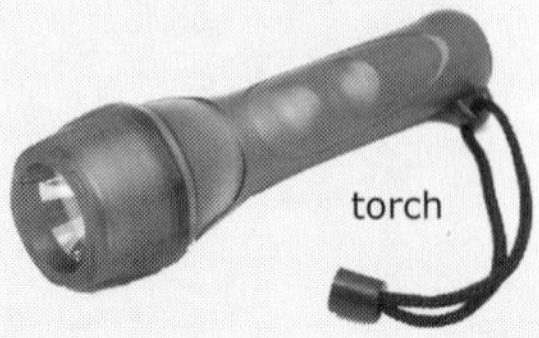

# EXPLORE Writing

9 *Preloved* is a site where you buy and sell things privately. Look at adverts a–d. Which item is ...

1 the newest? ☐
2 the oldest? ☐
3 the most expensive? ☐
4 the cheapest? ☐

PRELOVED CLASSIFIEDS FORUMS REVIEWS MEMBERS

**a** Aluminium folding bike

**Details**
Type: Private Advert
Price: £125

**Description**
I bought this bike about a year ago for £200 and have never used it, so it is brand new. It has 20″ wheels and 6 gears, plus a carry bag and a stand. £125 ono. I have more photos or you are welcome to view.

**b** Hohner Rockwood Electric Guitar

**Details**
Type: Private Advert
Price: £45

**Description**
I have a lovely Hohner Rockwood electric guitar complete with case. It's about 5 years old, and is in good condition with a few minor marks. I'm selling the guitar because I've moved on to a Les Paul guitar, but this one is ideal for a beginner! So grab yourself a bargain for only £45 – it cost me £400 brand new! Feel free to ask me any questions you have!
You can pay via cash or cheque if collecting.

**c** Lovely black and white male cat

**Details**
Type: Private Advert
Price: £30 no offers

**Description**
We are selling our much loved 2-year-old male cat. Due to our work commitments we cannot give him the love and time he needs. Would suit a family who can give him lots of affection. We will also give you his bed and feeding dishes.
Please no timewasters.

**d** Sofa for sale

**Details**
Type: Private Advert
Price: £325 ono

**Description**
White luxury Italian leather 3-seater sofa
Modern design, only 3 years old, very good condition. H78cm x W240cm x D98cm
Reluctant sale – we are selling it because it's too big for the sitting room in our new house!

10 There are some phrases and abbreviations which you often find in this type of ad. Match expressions 1–8 with meanings a–h.

1 private advert
2 brand new
3 ono
4 you are welcome to view
5 if collecting
6 no offers
7 no timewasters
8 reluctant sale

a I might accept a slightly lower price (= or near offer)
b if you come in person to take it away
c you can come to see it
d I have to sell it, but I don't really want to
e it's never been used, completely new
f don't contact me if you are not serious
g this is an ordinary person advertising, not a shop
h I won't accept a lower price

11 Which items include the following information? Tick (✓) the correct boxes.

| | Bicycle | Guitar | Cat | Sofa |
|---|---|---|---|---|
| A general description | | ✓ | | ✓ |
| Specific facts about the item, e.g. size | | | | |
| The condition of the item | | | | |
| Extras or accessories included | | | | |
| The reason the person is selling it | | | | |
| Who the item would be good for | | | | |

12 Think of something you would like to sell (or give away free!) on *Preloved* and write your advert. Try to include at least four of the points in Exercise 11.

# 8 Interview Nightmare journeys

**1** **Before you watch, think about a time when you were on a journey and ...**

a lost something.
b got lost.

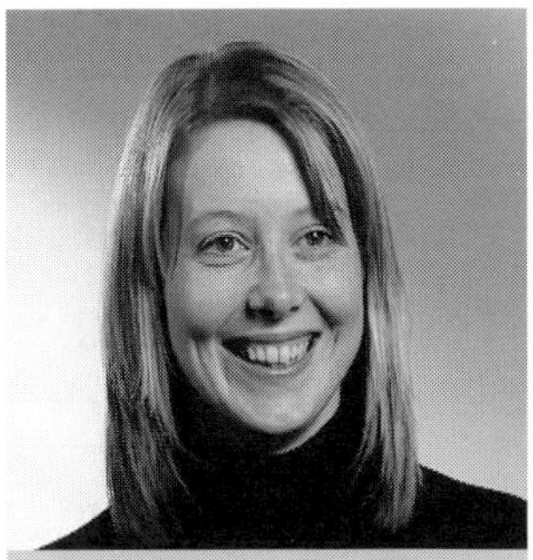
Clare

Andrés

**2** **Watch Clare and Andrés talking about their nightmare journeys. Which experience in Exercise 1 are they talking about, a or b?**

Clare: ______

Andrés: ______

**3** **Match the sentence halves to tell Clare's story. Watch again (0:11–1:47) to check.**

| | | | |
|---|---|---|---|
| 1 | They had to walk about 15 miles ... | a | because it was too wide. |
| 2 | They got lost ... | b | to signal for help. |
| 3 | They followed a river ... | c | when they arrived at the camp. |
| 4 | They couldn't cross the river ... | d | when they came to rescue them. |
| 5 | They climbed a hill ... | e | not realising they were on the wrong side of it. |
| 6 | They used their torches ... | f | because they weren't very good at reading the map. |
| 7 | Their teachers were angry ... | g | to see where they were. |
| 8 | Everyone else was asleep ... | h | carrying all their camping equipment. |

**4** **Clare uses the adverbs in brackets to emphasise these things she says. Put the adverbs in the correct position in the sentences. Watch again (0:11–1:47) to check.**

1 The group that we were in weren't good at map reading. (particularly)
2 We decided to follow a river, not realising that it made a difference which side of the river we were on. (really)
3 So at about 11 o'clock at night, we'd managed to get ourselves on top of a hill. (eventually)
4 We thought we could see what looked like the rest of our group camping down below, so we started signalling SOS on our torches and it was our group. (luckily)
5 Everybody had eaten, they were asleep, we had to pitch our tent and get up at five o'clock the next morning. (fast; still)

**5** **Are these statements about Andrés' story true or false? Watch again (1:52–2:54) to check.**

| | | |
|---|---|---|
| 1 | Andrés travelled from Florence to Vienna by bus. | TRUE / FALSE |
| 2 | Someone stole his money and documents. | TRUE / FALSE |
| 3 | He had €200 in his pocket. | TRUE / FALSE |
| 4 | He didn't know anyone in Vienna. | TRUE / FALSE |
| 5 | The Guatemalan embassy was open when he got there. | TRUE / FALSE |
| 6 | No one at the embassy knew how to help him. | TRUE / FALSE |
| 7 | They rang the Guatemalan embassy in the United States. | TRUE / FALSE |
| 8 | Andrés had to spend all his money on a new passport. | TRUE / FALSE |

**6** **Complete these extracts from Andrés' story with a correct preposition. Watch again (1:52–2:54) to check.**

1 I tied it __________ my waist.
2 I was __________ a passport, just with a hundred euros __________ my name.
3 I went, waited a couple __________ hours for them to open up the embassy.
4 __________ my surprise, the ambassador was __________ holiday and no one else knew what to do __________ that sort of situation.
5 They said just print him a new passport __________ €75.

**7** **Which of the two situations would you find more worrying? Why?**

## GLOSSARY

**hike** (verb): to go for a long walk in the countryside or hills
**backpack** (noun): a type of bag that you carry on your back
**pitch (a tent)** (verb): to choose a place for a tent and put it there
**waist** ( noun): the part around the middle of your body where you wear a belt
**stash** (verb): to keep something in a safe, secret place

# 9 Make up your mind

**VOCABULARY**
Problems in the home

**1** **Complete descriptions 1–4 of problems in the home and match them with the pictures a–d.**

a 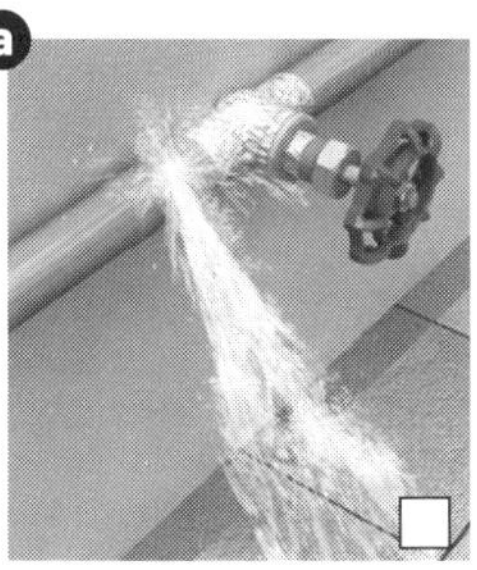
b 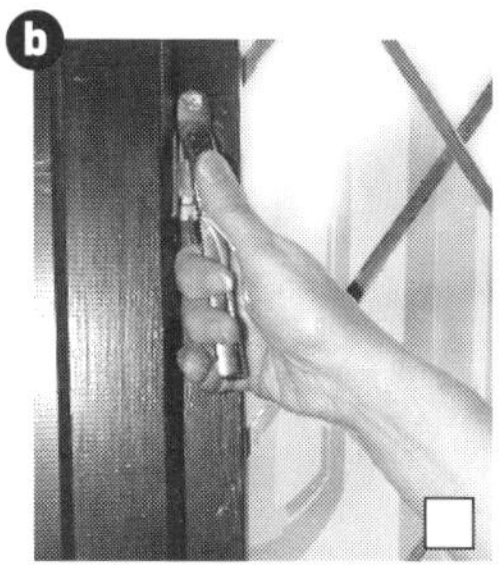
c 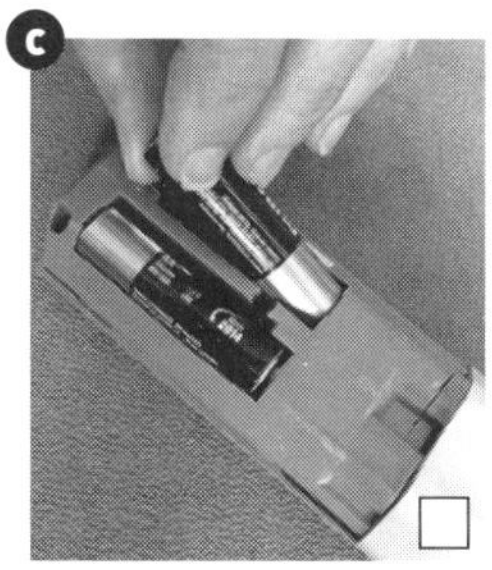
d 

1 There's a ___________ cut.
2 The ___________ are flat.
3 The ___________ 's burst.
4 The ___________ 's stuck.

**2** **Cross out the things that are *not* possible.**

1 The fridge / heating / handle isn't working.
2 The tap's stuck / flat / leaking.
3 The bathroom / pipe / floor is flooded.
4 The handle's come off / burst / stuck.
5 The shower / handle / toilet is leaking.

**VOCABULARY**
Discussing problems and solutions

**3** **Put the words in the correct order to complete the conversation.**

A OK, let's go. Oh!
B What's the matter?
A I've no idea. The door isn't opening.
B [1]try / I'll / it / give / a ___________ . No, you're right. I think the batteries are flat.
A Oh no. [2]we / what / to / are / going / do ___________ ?
B Can't you open it with the key?
A [3]a / I'll / go / have ___________ , but I don't think so. No, it only opens the boot. [4]shall / what / do / we ___________ ?
B [5]we'll / have / get / to ___________ new batteries, but I guess we have to go to the car dealer for that, and they won't be there at this time of night.
A [6]we're / to / well / going / to / have ___________ get the bus this evening, then I'll try to sort it out tomorrow.

**VOCABULARY**
Decision-making

**4** **Complete the article with verbs in the correct form.**

# Group Problem Solving

Do you have a problem at work? Try this 3-step approach to [1]ru__________ a meeting to [2]s__________ your problem collectively.

**1** Start by [3]br__________ ideas. Ask everyone to think freely and don't criticise. In this way, people can [4]l__________ to their hearts and [5]tr__________ their intuition, and not just [6]l__________ at the facts.

**2** Divide the group into smaller teams. Ask them to [7]c__________ up with plans and [8]dev__________ solutions to the problem.

**3** Come together again, and ask each team to report back on their discussion. You don't need to [9]m__________ a final decision instantly, but you should have plenty of ideas to think about.

**Over to you**

If you can, try this problem-solving technique with colleagues or friends. Write a paragraph evaluating how successful it was.

**GRAMMAR**
Real and unreal conditionals

**5** **Complete the sentences using the correct form of the verbs in the box.**

do feel go have (x2) know open see

1 If I __________ more time, I'd really like to go to yoga classes again.
2 If I __________ Frank tomorrow, I'll ask him about our reservation.
3 I __________ it this afternoon if I get back in time. OK?
4 If we __________ a new office, we'd need to take on a lot of extra staff. I don't know if it's such a good idea.
5 Are you OK? If you __________ sick, you really should go home.
6 If we __________ another room in our flat, we could invite people to stay.
7 We __________ away in December if we can afford it.
8 I'm sorry. If I __________ the answer, I'd tell you, but I really have no idea.

**VOCABULARY**
Negotiating

**6** **Complete the expressions in bold in the conversation using the words in the box.**

could how if just mean say that

A OK, so we need to get this report in by the end of the month. [1]__________ **about if** we write one section each?
B **But that would** [2]__________ there's a risk of it not fitting together very well at the end.
C Hm. **Or we could** [3]__________ make time to work on it all together.
B But it would be very time-consuming to work like that.
C Why don't we set up a wiki? [4]__________ **way**, we can all contribute to the whole report.
B **But** [5]__________ **we** do that, [6]__________ **we** please also get together sometimes? I think it's important to talk face to face.
A OK, so **let's** [7]__________ we work together on one section on the wiki, then meet again to discuss how it's going. Would next Tuesday be OK for you?

**VOCABULARY**
Dealing with conflict

**7 Match verbs 1–6 with the phrases a–f.**

1 resolve
2 show
3 have
4 argue
5 cause
6 reach

a a compromise
b a conflict
c someone respect
d an argument / a disagreement / a row
e your case
f tension

# MY English

**8 Read what Reiner says and choose the correct way to complete the sentence.**

In dealing with Italian companies, Reiner had to ...
a learn a different language.
b learn a different way of using English.

I work for a company which designs and installs green energy technology. We've worked a lot in the past with British companies and I'm used to speaking fairly directly to people in meetings and so on. We recently started dealing with some Italian companies, and I had some communication problems at first. Not for the language – we use English and my English is quite good – but I found that if I had to say anything slightly negative, it was often taken very personally and people became offended and defensive. So I had to learn to express myself in a more diplomatic, less direct way.

Reiner, Germany

# YOUR English

**9 Do you think people in your culture tend to be quite direct, or quite diplomatic?**

**10 Which sentence in each pair sounds more diplomatic, a or b?**

1 a I think you've made a mistake here.
  b I think maybe there's been a slight mistake here.

2 a We expect payment by the end of the month.
  b We would normally expect payment by the end of the month.

3 a We really need to start the meeting.
  b If you're ready, could we start the meeting?

4 a No, that's not what I meant.
  b No, I'm sorry. There seems to be a misunderstanding.

**11 Which of the more diplomatic sentences use(s) ...**

1 a modal verb? ___
2 a question instead of a statement? ___
3 an introductory phrase like *I'm afraid*? ___
4 a 'softening' word like *perhaps*? ___ , ___
5 an impersonal expression instead of a personal one? ___ , ___
6 an expression like *rather, a bit*? ___

# EXPLORE Reading

**12** **Edward De Bono, the inventor of the 'Six Thinking Hats' technique, also created 'lateral thinking'. This is a way of thinking creatively and finding new solutions to problems. Read the story from his organisation's website, which illustrates lateral thinking, and correct the errors in this summary.**

A farmer's daughter owed some money to a moneylender, but she said she would marry him instead of paying the debt. The girl liked the moneylender because he was young and handsome. The girl's father was not happy, so he suggested they should use a random game to decide what would happen. Her father put two stones in a bag and said that if the girl picked a white stone, she could marry the moneylender. But he cheated and put only black stones in the bag. The girl saw this and didn't know what to do.

**13** **Answer the questions.**

1 What happens if the girl picks a stone?
2 What happens if she refuses to pick a stone?

## Lesson in Lateral Thinking: The Story Of Two Stones

Many years ago in a small village, a farmer owed a large sum of money to a moneylender. The moneylender, who was old and ugly, liked the farmer's beautiful daughter. So he said he would forget the farmer's debt if he could marry his daughter. Both the farmer and his daughter were horrified by the proposal. So the clever moneylender suggested that they let chance decide. He told them that he would put a black stone and a white stone into an empty bag. Then the girl would have to pick one stone from the bag.

1 If she picked the black stone, she would have to marry the moneylender and her father's debt would be cancelled.
2 If she picked the white stone, she would not have to marry him and her father's debt would still be cancelled.
3 If she refused to pick a stone, her father would have to go to prison.

They were standing on a path in the farmer's field, full of stones. The moneylender bent down and picked up two stones. As he picked them up, the sharp-eyed girl noticed that he had picked up two black stones and put them into the bag. He then asked the girl to pick a stone from the bag.

Now, what would you do if you were the girl? If you had to advise her, what would you tell her?

Careful analysis would produce three possibilities:

1 The girl could refuse to take a stone.
2 The girl could show the two black stones in the bag and expose the moneylender's dishonesty.
3 The girl could pick a black stone and marry the old man to save her father.

The girl's dilemma cannot be solved with traditional logical thinking.

Click here to find out what the girl did.

**14** **When you have thought about the problem, read the end of the story at the bottom of the page and choose the best explanation (1–3).**

1 The girl tricked the moneylender. She made him believe she had picked a white stone, so she and her father were free.
2 The girl put the moneylender in a difficult moral position. He could not show he had used a dishonest trick, so he had to let the girl and her father go free.
3 The girl confused the moneylender, so she saved herself and her father.

The girl put her hand into the bag and took out a stone.
Without looking at it, she let it fall onto the path where it immediately became lost among all the other stones.
'Oh, silly me!' she said. 'But never mind, if you look into the bag for the one that is left, you will know which stone I picked.'
Since the remaining stone was black, she must have picked the white one.
And since the moneylender did not want to admit his dishonesty, the girl changed what seemed an impossible situation into an extremely positive one.
She looked beyond the obvious to find a solution. This is just one example of the power of Lateral Thinking.

# Documentary The hairdressing entrepreneurs 9

1 **Before you watch, read this book extract and circle the correct options in the summary below.**

> Men are changing, and expressions of male vanity are, without doubt, on the rise. Some say the male-grooming market is an industry worth $3.5 billion.
>
> It has become acceptable now for men to indulge in grooming; sales of 'beauty' products targeted at men have rocketed. In fact, they have increased at twice the rate as products aimed at women.

- Men are 1 more / less interested in taking care of their looks and are spending 2 more / less on cosmetics and beauty services than in the past.

2 **How acceptable is it where you live for men to be interested in beauty and personal grooming?**

Piero

Gabriela

3 **Watch the whole documentary and tick (✓) the best summary.**

1 Piero and Gabriela met when they did a marketing course together. They now have their own hair and beauty business and are opening a training school soon. ☐
2 Piero and Gabriela met when she was studying in the UK and set up a hair and beauty business together. In the future, they hope to have a training school. ☐
3 Piero and Gabriela met when she came to work in his hair salon. They are now partners in the business and have just opened a training school. ☐

4 **Are these statements true or false? Watch Part 1 (0:06–2:45) of the documentary to check.**

1 Piero came to the UK when he was 21. TRUE / FALSE
2 He has worked in hairdressing since he was a child. TRUE / FALSE
3 He wanted to offer some new services in his hairdressing salon. TRUE / FALSE
4 Gabriela came to the UK to study marketing. TRUE / FALSE
5 She helped Piero with the business aspects of his idea. TRUE / FALSE
6 She feels that working as a husband and wife team has advantages and disadvantages. TRUE / FALSE

5 **Circle the correct way to complete these sentences. Watch Part 2 (2:45–4:44) to check.**

1 The UK is quite advanced / traditional as regards marketing, but quite advanced / traditional when it comes to beauty and grooming.
2 Piero and Gabriela offer a quality service that makes people feel different / comfortable.
3 To meet their clients / standards, they need to invest / save a lot of money.
4 With the recession, they have had to cut / suspend some of their services.
5 They would like to train other people and open more salons / expand their services.

6 **Piero and Gabriela use some fixed expressions. Match verbs 1–9 with words and phrases a–i.**

| | |
|---|---|
| 1 come up with | a my ability |
| 2 look after | b from the crowd |
| 3 find | c money |
| 4 enjoy | d knowledge |
| 5 make | e a job |
| 6 improve | f comfortable |
| 7 make (someone) feel | g someone's company |
| 8 pass on | h someone |
| 9 stand out | i an idea |

**7** **Complete these extracts with verbs from Exercise 6. Watch again to check.**

**Piero**

1 The fact that I was already qualified when I came here helped me to ________________ a good job, so I could ________________ good money, so I could afford to travel.

2 So the experience I had of travelling helped me to ________________ some new ideas.

3 I was surrounded by hundreds of granddads ... I ________________ their company.

Piero

**Gabriela**

4 I decided to come here to ________________ my English.

5 I'm flexible to be able to ________________ my family.

6 We give a different service that ________________ people feel comfortable.

7 The next level is to have a school so I can train people and ________________ my knowledge to them.

8 My hopes for the future ... [it] will be nice to be able to teach people and train them in the way we work, and ________________ from the crowd.

Gabriela

**8** **Piero and Gabriela sometimes use the same word in different collocations. Complete these extracts. Each pair uses the same word.**

1 a I enjoyed their ___________, I enjoyed their traditional stories.
  b My role in the ___________ is quality control, bookkeeping, cleaning ...

2 a I did a ___________ degree in Mexico.
  b In certain aspects, UK is quite advanced, if you want to talk about from the ___________ point of view.

3 a We've slowly been making it ___________.
  b I'm flexible to be able to look after my family and ___________ at the same time.

**9** **Which words in Exercise 8 are used with a different meaning?**

___________, ___________

**10** **Complete the summary about Piero and Gabriela with these expressions about work. Watch again to check.**

business market quality control train apprenticeship recession qualified expand

Piero did his [1]________________ in Italy, so he was already [2]________________ when he came to the UK. When he met his wife, Gabriela, they set up a small [3]________________. Gabriela's role in the company includes [4]________________, bookkeeping, research and [5]________________ analysis. The current [6]________________ has meant they have had to cut down on some of the services they offer, but they hope to [7]________________ in the future and [8]________________ other people in their working practices.

**11** **Have you or has anyone you know set up a business? Was it successful? What difficulties were there at the beginning?**

## GLOSSARY

**apprenticeship** (noun): when someone learns the skills needed to do a job by working for someone who already has skills and experience
**grooming** (noun): the things that you do to make your appearance tidy and pleasant
**bookkeeping** (noun): the job or activity of keeping an exact record of the money that has been spent or received by a business or other organisation
**short back and sides** (noun): a traditional man's hairstyle that is very short at the back and sides of his head and slightly longer on top
**recession** (noun): a period when the economy of a country is not successful and conditions for business are bad

# 10 Impressions

**VOCABULARY**
Remembering an event

**1** Circle the correct words to complete the conversation.

**A** Did you see Inspector Morse last night?
**B** Yeah, it was good, wasn't it? And that [1]reminds / remembers me, did I tell you I saw them filming it a few weeks ago?
**A** Really? Did you [2]remember / recognise the actors?
**B** Not at first, no. I [3]can't / couldn't remember why I was in town that day … Ah yes, I [4]remember / remind, I was just coming back from the dentist when I [5]noticed / recognised a whole lot of police cars. At first, I thought there'd been an accident, but then I realised what it was.
**A** What were they filming?
**B** [6]I'd / I've forgotten exactly what was happening, but I [7]can remember / can forget them filming the same scene again and again. [8]Looking / Watching back, it was actually quite boring, nothing like the TV programme when you see it!

**GRAMMAR**
Verb patterns

**2** Complete the sentences with the correct form of the verb: *-ing*, *to* infinitive or past simple.

1 **I'll never forget** ___________ (meet) your father for the first time.
2 **I never remember** ___________ (charge) my mobile at night, so it's always run out in the morning when I need it.
3 **I can remember** the hotel where we ___________ (stay) on our honeymoon, but I don't remember its name.
4 **I forgot** ___________ (send) my sister a birthday message, and she was really upset.
5 **I've forgotten how** ___________ (access) my account. Can you remember?
6 **I completely forgot that** I ___________ (have) a dentist's appointment yesterday until they rang me this morning. I think they were a bit annoyed.
7 **I don't remember** ___________ (do) anything special for my birthday last year.
8 **I remember that** I ___________ (be) on holiday in the mountains when the Berlin Wall came down.

**Over to you**

Choose four or five of the sentence beginnings in Exercise 2 and write sentences that are true for you.

**VOCABULARY**
Problems with things you've bought

**3** **Match pictures a–d with problems 1–4.**

**a**
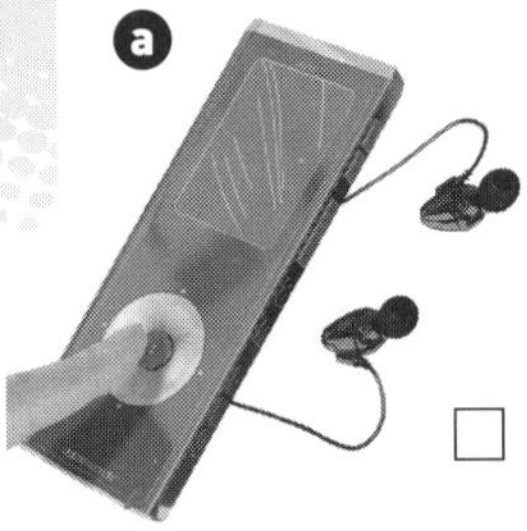
**b**

**c**
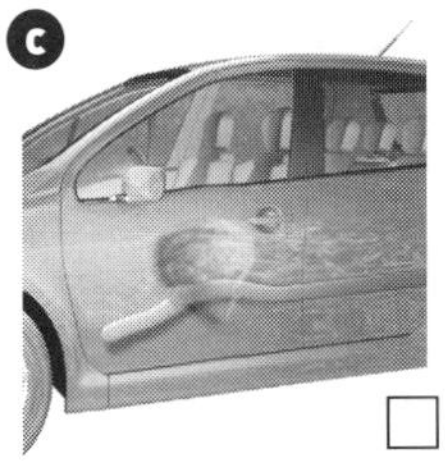
**d**

1 It's chipped and cracked.
2 It's faded.
3 It's scratched.
4 It's dented.

**4** **Cross out the word in each group that is *not* possible.**

1 The CD / screen / page is scratched.
2 The jacket / magazine / T-shirt is the wrong size.
3 The CD cover / plate / car is cracked.
4 The colour / T-shirt / magazine is torn.
5 The on-off switch / jacket / freezer doesn't work.

**GRAMMAR**
Present perfect simple and progressive

**5** **Complete these people's complaints using the present perfect simple or progressive form of the verbs in brackets.**

1 I ____________ (wait) to speak to someone for twenty minutes.

2 I ____________ (write) to you three times, but I ____________ (have) a reply.

3 I ____________ (stay) in your hotels for over five years, and this is the first time you ____________ (charge) me extra for breakfast.

4 I ____________ (try) to call you for the last two days, but your lines are always busy.

5 You ____________ (repair) my computer for two weeks now. I can't believe it's still not ready!

6 I ____________ (wait) for three weeks for the book I ordered from you. Can you tell me when it was sent?

7 I'm really not happy with the service your company ____________ (provide) this time.

8 I ____________ (try) all week to speak to your manager, but she's never available.

**VOCABULARY**
Softeners

**6** **Complete the softening expressions in this conversation.**

A Hi. Is it OK if I just leave these files on your desk for a moment?
B Well actually, **I've** $^{1}$**b____________ meaning to** talk to you about that.
A Oh yes?
B Yes. **It's** $^{2}$**j____________ that** I really need that space when I'm working.
A But it's only for a few minutes.
B Well, **to** $^{3}$**b____________ fair,** you often leave stuff on my desk for days at a time. It's **a** $^{4}$**b____________** annoying.
A But I don't have anywhere to put my stuff.
B Well, I'm sorry about that, but $^{5}$**t____________ be honest,** it's not my problem.
A OK, well, I'm sorry. I can see it's not very satisfactory. I'll ask if there's a free desk somewhere else.
B Thanks. If you could, **I'd** $^{6}$**r____________ appreciate it.**

# TimeOut

**7** **Complete the crossword about problems in the home, or with things you have bought.**

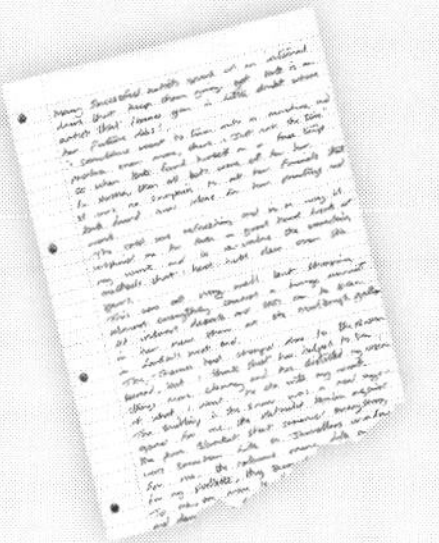

**ACROSS**

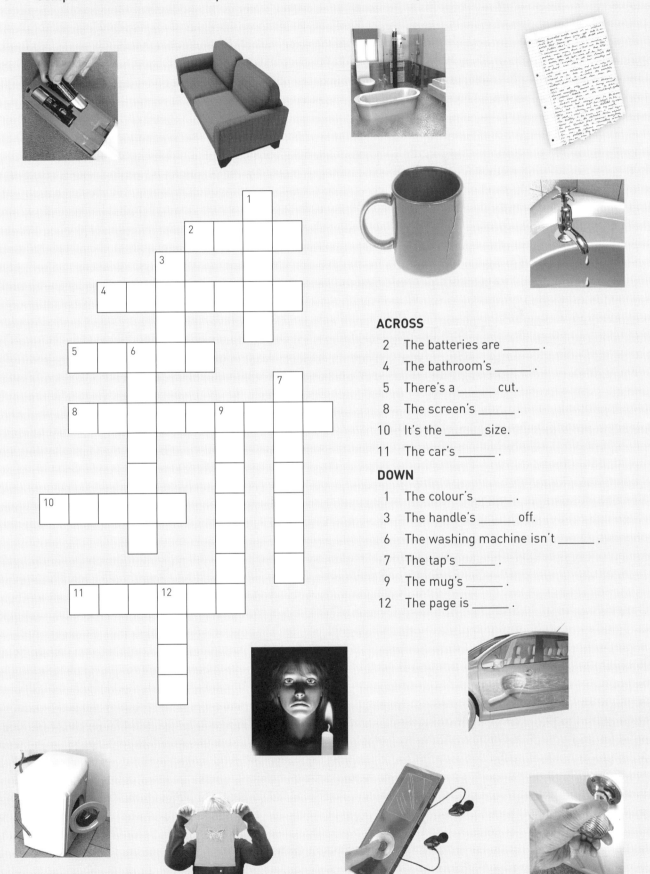

2 The batteries are ______ .
4 The bathroom's ______ .
5 There's a ______ cut.
8 The screen's ______ .
10 It's the ______ size.
11 The car's ______ .

**DOWN**

1 The colour's ______ .
3 The handle's ______ off.
6 The washing machine isn't ______ .
7 The tap's ______ .
9 The mug's ______ .
12 The page is ______ .

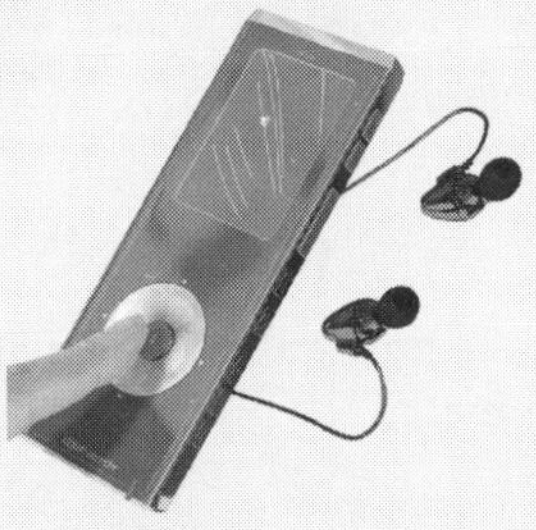
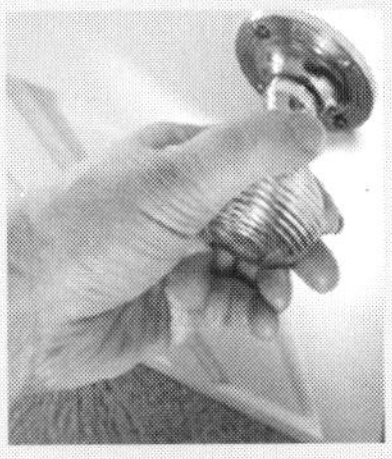

# EXPLORE Writing

**8** **Read the customer reviews (a–c) below of a hotel on a travel website.**

Which reviews complain about ...

1 the value for money offered by the hotel? ___ , ___
2 the location of the hotel? ___ , ___
3 the room they stayed in? ___ , ___
4 the cleanliness of the hotel? ___ , ___
5 the service in the hotel? ___ , ___

https://www.places_to_say.biz

**a** The hotel was **acceptable**, a bit too far from the centre of town, and a little **shabby**. The owner was quite **pleasant**. The only real drawback was the price – €95 seems **excessive**, considering it did not even include breakfast.

**b** Tiny room, **filthy** bathroom. Food OK but the service was very slow. Too expensive for the facilities offered and a long way from the beach.

**c** We had to wait over an hour for our room, which was small and rather **cramped** and had a strange smell. Perhaps this was something used to kill the mosquitoes – the walls were covered in squashed insect bodies. Towels from the 1950s, a TV that could only receive two channels. The staff were friendly enough, but this doesn't compensate for the very **poor** room.

**9** **Match the adjectives (1–7) used in the reviews with their meanings a–g.**

| | | | |
|---|---|---|---|
| 1 | acceptable | a | quite nice |
| 2 | shabby | b | old and in bad condition |
| 3 | pleasant | c | very dirty |
| 4 | excessive | d | small, with not enough space to move around |
| 5 | filthy | e | good enough, but not more than that |
| 6 | cramped | f | too expensive |
| 7 | poor | g | of very low standard |

**10** **Cross out the word in each group that *cannot* be described by the adjective.**

1 The service / food / receptionist / room was acceptable.
2 The room / building / furniture / food was shabby.
3 The hotel / receptionist / value / location was pleasant.
4 The service / room / bathroom / towel was filthy.
5 The bathroom / location / balcony / breakfast room was cramped.

**11** **You stayed in the same hotel and were not impressed. These are the ratings you gave.**

**Ratings**

| | | |
|---|---|---|
| Value | ●●○○○ | ___ |
| Location | ●●●○○ | ___ |
| Room | ●●○○○ | ___ |
| Cleanliness | ●○○○○ | ___ |
| Service | ●●●○○ | ___ |

**Make notes about the problems with each point, then write your review for the website.**

# Interview Witnessing a crime

1 Before you watch, think about these questions. Have you ever witnessed someone committing a crime or doing something dishonest? What happened? What did you do?

Carlos

Aurora

2 Watch Carlos and Aurora. Who …

a revealed a crime? ____________

b helped prevent a crime? ____________

3 Circle the correct details about Carlos' story. Watch again (0:11–1:58) to check.

It happened one [1]morning / afternoon in Madrid, when he was out [2]walking / jogging. He saw a man steal a woman's [3]purse / handbag and run away. He ran after the man because he wanted to [4]fight with him / stop him. He was just [5]three / five metres away from the man when [6]three / four other men appeared and all together they managed to stop the thief and get back the woman's money. It was the money she had earned in the last [7]week / month which she was sending to her family in [8]South Africa / South America.

4 Are these sentences about Aurora's story true or false? Watch again (2:03–2:43) to check.

1 Aurora's family were farmers in Puerto Rico. TRUE / FALSE
2 Her father and his friends killed and cooked a chicken for lunch. TRUE / FALSE
3 They stole the chicken from someone's house. TRUE / FALSE
4 The chicken belonged to Aurora's neighbour. TRUE / FALSE
5 Aurora told her mother what had happened. TRUE / FALSE

5 How do you think these people in the two stories felt? More than one answer may be possible.

embarrassed relieved guilty sorry angry proud grateful

1 Carlos: ____________
2 the woman whose money was stolen: ____________
3 Aurora: ____________
4 Aurora's neighbour: ____________
5 Aurora's parents: ____________

6 Carlos and Aurora use phrasal verbs to talk about what happened to them. Match phrasal verbs 1–6 with meanings a–f.

| | |
|---|---|
| 1 run away | a get possession again |
| 2 run around | b return |
| 3 take back | c escape |
| 4 grow up | d spend time as a child, become an adult |
| 5 come back | e run in circles |
| 6 run after | f chase |

7 Add the correct form of a phrasal verb from Exercise 6 to these extracts. Watch the video again to check.

1 Suddenly, the guy started to ______________.
2 I started to ______________ him.
3 I ______________ the money ______________.
4 When I was ______________ in the countryside …
5 There were a lot of chickens, always ______________.
6 When the neighbour ______________, I was very little, and I said …

8 How would you have reacted in the two situations?

# 11 Truth and lies

**VOCABULARY**
Verbs of communication

**1** **Match what the people are saying (1–7) with the verbs of communication (a–g) below.**

1. Have you heard about Bill and Katrina? Apparently, they've split up and she's gone back to Poland! [f]

2. My daughter finds her school lessons much too easy. She's always been clever for her age. [ ]

3. Hey you! Yes, you! Get out of here – this is private property! [ ]

4. Sshh, talk quietly. The baby's sleeping. [ ]

5. **A** Has the number 14 been?
   **B** No, it's always the same with the buses, isn't it? You wait for 25 minutes, then three come all together. [ ]

6. **A** I never said that!
   **B** Yes, you did. I distinctly remember. [ ]

7. Aagh! Oh, you gave me such a shock! I didn't hear you coming. [ ]

a whisper
b complain
c boast
d scream
e argue
f gossip
g shout

**VOCABULARY**
Relating a conversation

**2** Cross out the expression in each group that is *not* correct.

So we were talking about the traffic and [1]I said / I said to him / I said him, 'I'm thinking of getting a bike and cycling to work.' And then [2]he went / he say / he goes, 'I can't ride a bike, actually.' And [3]I'm like / I like / I was like, 'You're joking!' And [4]he says to me / he said / he saying, 'No, seriously. I grew up in the mountains and I just never learned.' So [5]I goes / I go / I say, 'OK, I'll teach you.' So we're both going to buy bikes next weekend. I'm slightly regretting it, actually.

**Over to you**
Describe a conversation you've had recently and record yourself using the DVD-ROM.

**GRAMMAR**
Reporting speech

**3** Circle the correct verbs to complete the conversation.

| | |
|---|---|
| THEO | Anyway, I hadn't written this essay for Dr Patel and when she [1]asked / told me why she hadn't received it, I [2]told / explained that I'd been ill. |
| KASIA | Were you? |
| THEO | No, but I had to [3]tell / say something. It was a bit embarrassing, really. She was really nice and [4]asked / told me if I was OK now. |
| KASIA | What did she [5]say / ask about the essay? |
| THEO | Well, she [6]explained / agreed to give me extra time, but she [7]said / told that I have to give it to her on Monday morning at the latest. |
| KASIA | What did you [8]say / tell? |
| THEO | I [9]explained / promised to do it, of course. So that's my weekend gone! |

**VOCABULARY**
Exchanging news

**4** Complete the expressions in bold using the correct forms of the verbs in the box.

hear (x4) say (x2) speak (x2) tell

| | |
|---|---|
| ANA | **Have you** [1]__________ **to** Kurt **lately**? |
| JENS | No. **Someone** [2]__________ he's moved to the Quito office. |
| CARLOS | **Who** [3]__________ **you that**? |
| JENS | I can't remember, but **I** [4]__________ it at the conference last week. |
| ANA | **That's not what I** [5]__________. I thought he was going to Caracas. |
| JENS | **Who** [6]__________ **that**? |
| ANA | I think it was Teresita. **Did you** [7]__________ **about her** move, by the way? |
| JENS | Yes. **Has anyone** [8]__________ **from her** since she left? |
| CARLOS | Yeah, **I** [9]__________ **to** her last week. She's good. |

## VOCABULARY
Upbringing

Sonia, Ireland

**5** **Sonia is talking about growing up in Ireland. Complete the expressions in bold.**

I **was** [1]**b**__________ **u**__________ in a small town in the south-west of Ireland. If we wanted to go to university, we **were** [2]**f**__________ **to** leave home, because the nearest university was over a hundred miles away. We **were** [3]**en**__________ **to** leave home when we left school or university, but **it was** [4]**un**__________ **to** live with your boyfriend or girlfriend before you were married. If we continued to live at home when we were working, we **were** [5]**ex**__________ **to** pay some 'rent' to contribute to the household expenses. Now I think things are a bit different. Parents and children have a more relaxed relationship. Kids **are** [6]**h**__________ **to** live for longer with their parents, but at the same time **it's** [7]**ac**__________ **to** live with your partner without being married.

# MY English

**6** **Read what Matti says about using English for work and say if these statements are true or false.**

1 Matti had problems explaining his ideas in English. TRUE / FALSE
2 He has learned to use a different style of conversation when speaking English. TRUE / FALSE

When I started working with colleagues from different countries, I was very happy to have the chance to use my English. But I was surprised when people kept saying, 'Are you OK?' or asking if I understood – when I was fine! It was my boss who explained that we Finns are happier with silence than speakers of other languages; we don't feel the need to always go 'Yes, yes,' or 'OK, fine', or whatever! But I've learned to do that more, and I also try to think of some comments or questions I can use to 'fill the silence' and start a new topic of conversation.

Matti, Finland

## YOUR English

**7** **In conversation in your language, is it more usual to leave silences or to 'fill the silence' with words like 'Yes, yes' or 'OK, fine'?**

**8** **Think of a conversation starter – a comment or question – that you could use about ...**

1 the weather
2 the journey here today
3 your day up to now
4 something funny/light-hearted you've heard in the news recently.

# EXPLORE Reading

'My friend told me this terrible story about her friend's grandmother. Apparently, her little dog went out in the rain and got really wet, so the old lady put him in the microwave for a couple of minutes to dry him out. You can imagine what happened ...'

**9 Read the anecdote and answer the question.**

Have you heard this story before? Where did you hear it? Do you believe it?

**10 The anecdote in Exercise 9 is an example of an 'urban legend'. Read this article about urban legends. Who says these things: Heather Whipps (HW); Mikel Koven (MK) or Jan Brunvand (JB)?**

1 Urban legends are often spread via the Internet. ______
2 Urban legends often have a sort of moral lesson or message. ______
3 It's very hard to discover how urban legends start. ______ , ______
4 Urban legends continue to be created and circulated. ______ , ______
5 Many people believe urban legends have some basis in fact. ______ , ______
6 Urban legends give us useful information about society. ______

## Urban Legends: How They Start and Why They Persist

**By Heather Whipps**

***My mother has this friend whose daughter ...***

Sound familiar? You might have heard the same story. Except that it was someone's boyfriend's brother – or friend's cousin. Or it's an urban legend.

Urban legends are an important part of popular culture, experts say, offering insight into our fears and the state of society. They're also good fun.

**The making of a legend**

Like the variations in the stories themselves, folklorists all have their own definitions of what makes an urban legend. Academics disagree on whether urban legends are too fantastic to be true, or at least partly based on fact, says Mikel J. Koven, a folklorist at the University of Wales.

Urban legends aren't easily verifiable. Usually passed on by word of mouth or – more commonly today – in email form, they often use the famous 'it happened to a friend of a friend' (or FOAF) clause that makes finding the original source of the story virtually impossible.

However, this isn't as important as the lessons they teach us, experts say.

'The lack of verification in no way diminishes the appeal that urban legends have for us,' writes Jan Harold Brunvand in *The Vanishing Hitchhiker: American Urban Legends and Their Meanings* (W. W. Norton & Company, 1981). The definition of an urban legend, he writes, is 'a strong basic story-appeal, a foundation in actual belief, and a meaningful message or moral.'

**Legends need to make cultural sense**

Koven thinks urban legends are also good indicators of current society. 'By looking at what's implied in a story, we get an insight into the fears of a group in society,' he told *LiveScience*. It's these fears that tend to give rise to new legends, he said.

**A lot of fun, too ...**

But urban legends aren't all serious, with the most believable ones often presented as funny stories, and Brunvand argues that legends should be around as long as there are inexplicable curiosities in life.

'It might seem unlikely that urban legends would continue to be created in an age of widespread literacy, rapid mass communications and restless travel,' he wrote in *The Vanishing Hitchhiker*, printed many years before widespread use of the Internet. 'A moment's reflection, however, reminds us of the many weird, fascinating but unverified rumors that often come to our ears – madmen on the loose, shocking personal experiences, unsafe products and many other unexplained mysteries of daily life.'

**11 Choose the best meaning, a or b, for these quotations from the article.**

1 'The lack of verification in no way diminishes the appeal that urban legends have for us.'
 a We enjoy urban legends because we know they are not true.
 b We don't mind if urban legends are true or not; we enjoy them anyway.
2 'By looking at what's implied in a story, we get an insight into the fears of a group in society.'
 a Urban legends are often about things that people are worried about.
 b Urban legends are often scary or frightening stories.
3 'It might seem unlikely that urban legends would continue to be created in an age of widespread literacy, rapid mass communications and restless travel.'
 a Urban legends seem too primitive for our modern society.
 b Urban legends spread easily because of modern communications.

**Over to you**

**Have you heard the story of the 'vanishing hitchhiker'? If not, you can find it online. Try to find some other examples of urban legends.**

# 11 Interview Family customs

1 **Before you watch, think about this question. In your culture, what are people's attitudes towards their parents and to older people in general?**

Imelda

Nishadi

Darren

2 **Watch the video. Which issue do all the speakers talk about?**

a family relationships
b attitudes towards older people
c differences between cultures

3 **Watch Imelda again. Which of these gestures might you see children using in Indonesia with an older person? Watch again (0:11–0:45) to check.**

a touching the elder's hand to their forehead
b kissing the elder's hand
c using a Western-style handshake
d all of the above

4 **Are these statements about Nishadi true or false? Watch again (0:50–2:17) to check.**

1 In Sri Lanka, it is very unusual for people to live with their parents after they are married. TRUE / FALSE
2 Parents' and children's lives are very closely integrated. TRUE / FALSE
3 Nishadi noticed that children were more independent at a younger age in the United States. TRUE / FALSE
4 Nishadi's parents are happy for her to have a part-time job. TRUE / FALSE
5 On balance, Nishadi likes the close relationship she has with her parents. TRUE / FALSE

5 **Darren talks about his family. Complete the information. Watch again (2:21–3:03) to check.**

Darren's parents grew up in Malta, but they moved to [1]______________ in the late [2]19___s. They had three children, two [3]______________ and a [4]______________ ; the oldest of these is now nearly [5]______________ years old.

6 **Complete these extracts about relationships with people using the words in the box.**

always around due for on since throughout towards

1 Parents know what is happening in their children's lives ___________ their lives. ☐
2 Life was, and still is, focused very much ___________ the family. ☐
3 There is a lot of respect ___________ elders. ☐
4 Life is very much about the parents and respect ___________ your parents and the family. ☐
5 There's ___________ somebody to go and talk to. ☐
6 ___________ to the Western influences things have changed. ☐
7 There's always somebody who has known you ___________ your birth. ☐
8 I'm still very dependent ___________ my parents. ☐

7 **Can you remember who said the extracts in Exercise 6? Write I, N or D. Watch again to check.**

8 **What similarities or differences are there between these cultures and your own?**

## GLOSSARY

**elders** (noun): the older, more respected people in a family or group
**forehead** (noun): the part of your face between your eyes and your hair
**support oneself** (verb): to be financially independent
**integrate** (verb): to become part of a group or society
**insistent** (adjective): firmly saying that something is true or must be done

# 12 Any questions?

VOCABULARY
Organising a talk

**1 Complete these extracts from a talk about yoga courses using the words in the box.**

| | | | | | |
|---|---|---|---|---|---|
| all | any | are | finally | further | going to |
| move on | start with | talk about | there | | |

1 Today, I'm [1]__________ [2]__________ the yoga courses we offer at our centre.
2 To [3]__________ , I'll describe briefly the different types of yoga.
3 First of [4]__________ , it's important to wear loose, comfortable clothes.
4 I'm going to [5]__________ now to talk about breathing techniques.
5 [6]__________ [7]__________ any questions?
6 And [8]__________ , I'd like to invite you to our demonstration lesson next Friday.
7 So, thank you for listening. [9]__________ [10]__________ questions?

VOCABULARY
Polite requests and questions

**2 Complete the questions with appropriate verbs.**

1 Would you __________ if I closed the door?
2 Could you __________ me your views on the election result?
3 Could I __________ you a favour?
4 Could I ask you what you __________ about my proposal?
5 __________ you mind passing me the water?
6 Could I ask you to __________ something for me?
7 __________ you tell me a little bit about the course?

**3 Which questions (1–7) in Exercise 2 ...**

a ask for an opinion or information? ___ , ___ , ___
b do you say before you ask someone to do something? ___ , ___
c ask someone to do something? ___
d ask for permission? ___

**GRAMMAR**
Indirect questions

**4** Make these questions more polite using *Could I ask you ...? / Could you tell me ...?*

**1**
a Which bank do you have an account with?
b Are you satisfied with the service?

**2**
a How often do you go to your nearest supermarket?
b Are you happy with the range of products offered?

**3**
a Do you ever go to the cinema?
b How many films do you see in a year?

**4**
a Do you use the public transport in this area?
b How efficient is the service?

**5**
a How many cafés or restaurants are there in your area?
b Do you eat out more for lunch, or dinner?

## Over to you

Choose the questions in one or two of the sections in Exercise 4 and record your answers using the DVD-ROM.

**VOCABULARY**
Answering questions at a talk

**5** Add the words in the box to the speaker's answers.

a an back can it ~~know~~ out ~~to~~

1 How many different types of yoga are there?
To be honest, **I don't** *know* **the answer** *to* **that**.

2 When did people first start practising yoga?
**That's good question.**

3 What kind of yoga is best for me?
Well, **depends** why you want to do it.

4 How do I know if I'll enjoy yoga?
**All I say is**, you'll certainly feel better!

5 Will there be beginners and advanced students in the same class?
**That's important point**.

6 Can I pay in monthly instalments?
I'm not sure, but **I'll find for you.**

7 Can you tell me if there are still places in the lunchtime class?
I need to check that, but **I'll get to you** tomorrow.

# TimeOut

6 A lot of jokes in English use a question/answer format. Can you match up the questions and answers to make these jokes? Which joke(s) do you like best?

1 What do ghosts have for dessert?

2 Why is six afraid of seven?

3 Why didn't the skeleton go to the dance?

4 Where do cows go to have fun?

5 What time is it when an elephant sits on your chair?

6 Why did the fly dance on top of the jar of jam?

7 Which two English words have the most letters in them?

8 Why do birds fly south?

a Because he had no body to go with.

b Because it said 'Twist to open'.

c Because it's too far to walk.

d To the mooovies.

e It's time to get a new chair.

f Ice scream.

g Because 7, 8, 9. (seven 'ate' nine)

h Post office.

## Over to you

Find some more question/answer jokes on the Internet and practise telling them to people!

# EXPLORE Writing

**7** **Aia is giving a short talk in her English class about crossword puzzles. Here is an extract from her talk. Which slide would be better to go with this section, a or b? Why?**

'Today, I'm going to talk to you about something I enjoy doing – crossword puzzles. Modern crosswords have quite a short history, only about a hundred years, but they developed from an older type of word puzzle, the word square. We know that these were popular in 19th-century England, especially for children, but an example of one in Latin was even found in Pompeii, in the ruins of the ancient Roman city destroyed in the year 79AD.'

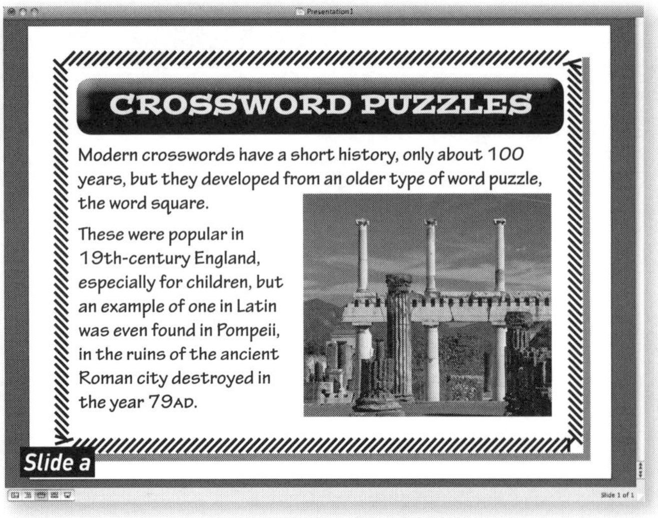


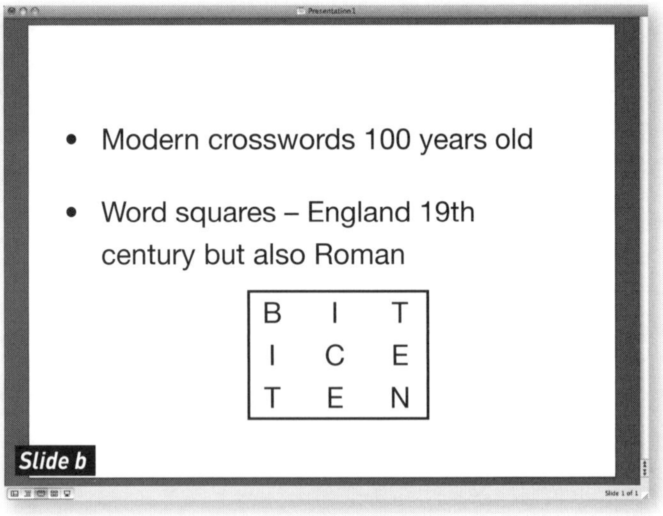

Modern crosswords 100 years old
Word squares – England 19th century but also Roman
B I T
I C E
T E N
Slide b


**8** **Circle the best advice about preparing slides for a presentation.**

**Good presentation slides should ...**

1 contain all the information in the talk / contain the main points of the talk
2 use complete sentences and paragraphs / use note form, abbreviations and bullet points.
3 have a lot of white space around the text / be covered completely with the text
4 use a lot of colours and special effects / not use distracting special effects.

**9** **Read the next section of Aia's talk and complete her slide.**

'The first modern crossword puzzle is generally considered to have been the one that was created by an Englishman, Arthur Wynne, and published in the *New York World* magazine in 1913. It was called a 'word-cross', but soon this was changed to the word we now use – crossword. Crosswords immediately became very popular all over America, and the first ones appeared in British magazines and newspapers in the early 1920s.'

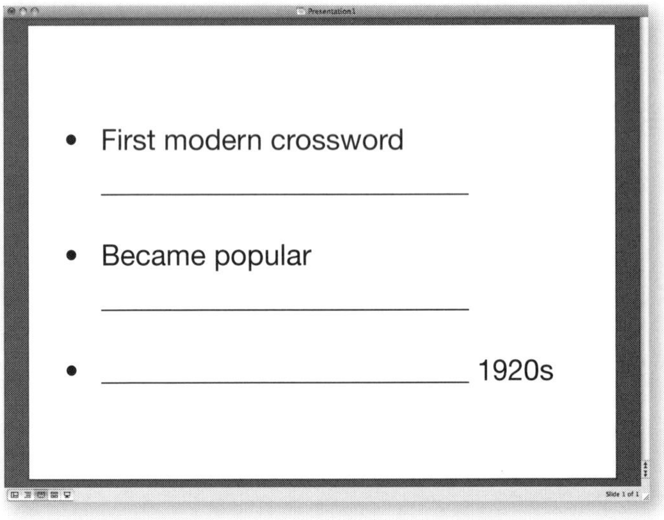


**10** **Prepare three or four slides for the talk you gave on coursebook p95 or on an interest you have.**

1 Before you watch, think about the advice you would give to someone who had to do a presentation or talk to a large group of people.

2 Watch Andrés and Ehi talking about giving presentations. Who mentions these things? Write A or E.

1 practising your presentation ☐
2 keeping your presentation lively ☐
3 using drama ☐
4 noting down the key points and sticking to them ☐
5 asking the audience questions ☐
6 using technology ☐
7 using your adrenalin rush positively ☐

Andrés

Ehi

3 Are these statements about Andrés true or false? Watch again (0:11–1:15) to check.

1 He first spoke in public 12 years ago. TRUE / FALSE
2 His father worked for a software company. TRUE / FALSE
3 The company wanted to show how easy their system was to use. TRUE / FALSE
4 He has never given a presentation since that time. TRUE / FALSE

4 Circle the correct option in these sentences about Ehi. Watch again (1:20–2:10) to check.

1 She works as a volunteer / trains volunteers.
2 She prepares people to talk to community groups / commercial companies.
3 She thinks there is / isn't only one way to give a good presentation.
4 She uses / doesn't use PowerPoint.

5 Circle the words Andrés and Ehi use in these comments about presentations. Watch again to check.

**Andrés**
1 People get very nervous / anxious when they have to speak to / in front of an audience.
2 I had to speak in front of an audience / auditorium of 3,500 people.
3 Make a note / list of the points you need to cover.
4 Try to rehearse / practise in front of anyone who / whoever is available.
5 Try to focus / channel that rush, the adrenalin you get before you open your mouth / speak.
**Ehi**
6 There's no hard-and-fast / rigid rule as to how to present or give a presentation.
7 I use other technologies like PowerPoint and stuff / things like that but also bring in / use some drama and some actions to keep the situation and the presentation very lively.

6 What do you think of the advice Andrés and Ehi gave?

## GLOSSARY

**user-friendly** (adjective): something that is easy to use or understand
**auditorium** (noun): the part of a large hall where people sit for a conference or concert
**rehearse** (verb): to practise something in order to prepare for a performance
**adrenalin** (noun): a substance that your body produces when you are angry, excited or frightened which makes your heart beat faster
**roller coaster** (noun): a fast and exciting ride in a fairground or amusement park that goes up and down very steep slopes
**workshop** (noun): when a group of people meet to learn more about something by discussing it and doing practical exercises

# 13 Looking back

**VOCABULARY**
Events in business

**1** **Complete the magazine article using the expressions in the box. Put the verbs in the correct form.**

| |
|---|
| bankrupt   build up   fire   resign   run   set up   take over (x2) |

## Small is beautiful

Mahesh Bhatt started working in the clothing industry at 15 years old. He got off to a bad start. He was 1__________ from his first job when he was rude to the manager, but did well in his next job and, after a few years, he 2__________ the company from the owners. Over the next 35 years, he 3__________ the small business into a successful chain of factories and shops. He 4__________ from the company at the age of 54, when it was 5__________ by an American group.

By an ironic twist, his brother Sameer went 6__________ soon afterwards, after investing his money in the same American company, which had then failed. The two brothers 7__________ a small business selling original designs in luxury fabrics. They 8__________ it with a small staff of three people, and are doing well.

'We are older, wiser and happier now,' says Mahesh. 'For us, small really is beautiful.'

**GRAMMAR**
*should have, could have*

**2** **Complete what the people say about things they regret in their working lives. Use *should have* or *could have* and the verbs in brackets.**

Ruth, England

**1** I *could have gone* (go) to university when I left school, but I decided to get a job instead. Now I'm 35, and I'm working part-time while I study for a law degree. It's hard work studying when you're older and working, too. I ______________ (not refuse) my university place when I was 18.

Corrado, Italy

**2** I'm a civil engineer, and in my first job I was asked to work in Saudi Arabia for two years. I refused because my wife was expecting our first child. I ______________ (accept) the job; I ______________ (earn) a lot of money to support my family, and I would have been promoted by now, too, with that extra experience.

Manoel, Brazil

**3** When I left university, I ______________ (join) my uncle in his business, but I wanted to get some experience first. I came to work for this multinational corporation, but I'm unhappy and stressed in my job. I ______________ (go) to work with my uncle, but I missed the opportunity, and he's taken on someone else now.

**Over to you**

Write about some things you regret in your work or education.

**VOCABULARY**
Acts of kindness and bravery

**3 Complete the expressions in bold in the stories.**

1 Nine-year-old Freddy Cicotti from Swansea, South Wales, **[1]ris___________ his life [2]b___________** jumping into a river in November to **[3]sa___________** a dog **from** drowning. The dog belonged to 78-year-old Myfanwy Evans, who later gave him £100 to **[4]th___________** him **for [5]res___________** the animal. 'I live alone and only have my dog for company,' she explained. 'I would have been devastated if he'd drowned.'

2 Annabel Leary, aged 14, was amazed when an elderly neighbour **[6]le___________** her a small sum of money when she died. 'I don't deserve it,' she said, 'I just enjoy spending time with the old people round here. I was really sad when Mavis died.' Despite suffering from an illness which often makes her tired and weak, Annabel is known in her area for **[7]th___________ing of** other people before herself. She **[8]he___________** her neighbours with their household chores and does constant small **[9]fav___________ for** them.

**GRAMMAR**
Unreal conditionals: past

**4 Complete the sentences with the correct form of the verbs in brackets to make unreal past conditional sentences.**

1 Why didn't you ask me? I ___________ (help) you if I ___________ (know) you were having difficulty.
2 If he ___________ (not be) sick as a child, he ___________ (not start) writing poems and songs.
3 If he ___________ (come) to the meeting yesterday, I ___________ (ask) him.
4 I ___________ (finish) by now if my computer ___________ (not crash) this morning.
5 If we ___________ (stay) in Montreal, the kids ___________ (grow up) speaking French as well as English.
6 I ordered this book on the Internet, but I ___________ (not buy) it if I ___________ (see) it first. It's really boring.
7 I ___________ (not tell) him if I ___________ (know) he was going to be so upset.
8 If you ___________ (not eat) so much yesterday, you ___________ (not have) difficulty sleeping.

**VOCABULARY**
Evaluating past actions

**5 Freya and Ben are having an argument. Complete the expressions in bold in the conversation.**

FREYA Is this the hotel? It looks pretty bad. And you **could have [1]t___________ me** it was over a garage.
BEN Well, **if I'd [2]k___________** where it was, obviously I'd have told you. The photo on the website wasn't very clear.
FREYA We **[3]___________ have known** it would be awful. It was really cheap.
BEN Maybe it **would have been [4]b___________ to** pay a bit more for something nicer.
FREYA Well, **if you'd [5]a___________ me**, that's what I'd have said, but you insisted on booking this place!

**VOCABULARY**
*make, let, be allowed to, be supposed to*

Patty, Italy

**6** **Complete what Patty says about cycling with these expressions.**

let you   make you   you're not allowed to   you're supposed to

When I first arrived in England, I used to ride my bike to work and I realised I was cycling in a very Italian way. I mean, I know 1_______________ ride on the pavement or the wrong way up a one-way street, but in general in Italy people 2_______________ do things like that if you're not causing any danger. In England, they 3_______________ get off your bike if you're doing that. And of course, 4_______________ have lights on your bike, but in Italy no one cares if you don't. Here in England, I got stopped by a police officer and given a fine for not having lights!

# MY English

**7** **Read what Abdou says and circle the correct way to complete this statement.**

Abdou feels more comfortable communicating in English face to face / in writing.

I come from Fez, where I've always worked as a tourist guide, showing visitors around my amazing city. I use English mainly, but also my first two languages, Arabic and French, sometimes. Tourism has developed here a lot in the last few years, and I've got a new and better job in a travel agency. As a guide, I needed to have very good spoken English, but now I have to do a lot of writing – things like reports and press releases as well as emails – and I'm finding it quite hard. I realise I'm not very sure about the correct grammar and it's hard when I have to write in a more formal style. I'm hoping to do a short course in writing skills in Cairo next year.

Abdou, Morocco

## YOUR English

**8** **Do you feel more comfortable communicating in English face to face with people, or in writing?**

**9** **Look at this table comparing speaking and writing. Tick (✓) the points that are not a problem for you, and put a cross (✗) against the points that you find difficult.**

| Speaking to someone face to face | | Writing to someone | |
|---|---|---|---|
| • You can express your ideas immediately, but you don't have much time to think before you speak. | ☐ | • You normally have time to think and plan before you write and as you are writing. | ☐ |
| • Your pronunciation has to be clear. | ☐ | • Your handwriting/typing and punctuation have to be clear. | ☐ |
| • Small grammar and vocabulary mistakes don't normally cause problems. | ☐ | • Your grammar and vocabulary need to be quite correct. | ☐ |
| • If someone doesn't understand, you can normally stop and clarify. | ☐ | • If someone doesn't understand what you've written, it's difficult or sometimes impossible to clarify. | ☐ |
| • You don't normally have to speak in a very formal way. | ☐ | • You quite often need to use more formal language. | ☐ |

**10** **Would you prefer to write or speak to someone in these situations?**

– to invite someone you don't know well to dinner
– to ask a company if they have any job vacancies
– to apologise to a colleague for a mistake you've made
– to tell a teacher you want to leave their course
– to tell your family you are getting married

# EXPLORE Reading

**YOKO ONO**

FACT FILE

- Born 1933
- Educated Japan and New York
- Artist since 1960s, often controversial and criticised
  - performance and conceptual art
  - experimental film
  - experimental and electronic music
- Activist for peace and human rights
- Married to Beatle, John Lennon

**11** What do you know about the artist, Yoko Ono? Read the information on the left. Did you learn anything new?

**12** Read the magazine article and match the opening sentences and phrases (1–6) with the gaps in paragraphs A–M.

**13** In which paragraph(s) do we understand that ...

1 Yoko Ono is a busy and active woman. ___
2 She remembers the moment she was born. ___
3 She investigates carefully before contributing her money or time to anything. ___
4 Journalists have often written negative things about her. ___, ___
5 She appreciates the experience of getting older. ___

**14** What is your impression of Yoko Ono?

She seems sincere / interesting / unpleasant / brave / disappointed / happy / unhappy / something else?

1 **The computer is my favourite invention.** ☐
2 **I was amazed to win the lifetime achievement Golden Lion ...** ☐
3 **Marriage is a difficult project.** ☐
4 **I don't have a favourite song from my back catalogue.** ☐
5 **The thing that would most improve my life ...** ☐
6 **Women are saying let's forget about feminism ...** ☐

## This much I know

**Yoko Ono, artist, 76, looks back on the lessons life has taught her.**

**A** **When I think of Japan, I think of food.** I miss the Japanese spirit, the culture and civilisation that we had and lost.

**B** ______________________ When seven years have passed and all your body's cells have been replaced, you're meant to experience that seven-year itch. John and I found that at that point our marriage got a lot better.

**C** **When I became 70 I started to see that every week I was learning something.** I'm very thankful: if I'd died 10 years ago I would have died dumb.

**D** ______________________ [at the 2009 Venice Biennale art festival]. I do read reviews, and the critics have not always been so nice.

**E** **I get requests from charities every week.** Deciding which to agree to is how I am educated.

**F** ______________________ I think all of them have something good about them. If you are creating something to share with the world, you have to believe that.

**G** ______________________ I feel lucky to be part of the global village. I don't mean to boast, but I'm so fast with technology. People think it all seems too much, but we'll get used to it. I'm sure it all seemed too much when we were learning to walk.

**H** **My earliest memory** is of the day of my birth, and looking at surgical instruments in an operating theatre. Many people do remember their births, but they deny it.

**I** ______________________ because they've seen that other women are not protective of you and you stand alone.

**J** **My son Sean was so protective of me** when he co-produced my new album; he wants it to be a success. His generation is extremely professional about music; mine is very instinctual.

**K** ______________________ is 27 hours in a day. I could meet all my deadlines.

**L** **Young people understand my work.** I don't know why. It's a mystery. Maybe the vibration of my work is together with the vibration of the universe now.

**M** **I don't mind if no one remembers me.** If I'm going to be remembered by all the fiction the press wrote about me, why would I want to be remembered at all?

# 13 Interview We all make mistakes

**1** **Before you watch, think about these questions. Have you ever made an embarrassing mistake at work? What did you do? What happened?**

Nishadi

Bắc

**2** **Watch Nishadi and Bắc. Who talks about these things? Write N, B or both.**

1 confusing instructions ______
2 not recognising someone ______
3 forgetting to do something ______

**3** **Are these statements about Nishadi true or false? Watch again (0:11–1:12) to check.**

1 Nishadi had never made a mistake with money before. TRUE / FALSE
2 She forgot to ask the customer for money. TRUE / FALSE
3 The manager noticed her mistake. TRUE / FALSE
4 The manager was angry with Nishadi. TRUE / FALSE
5 He cancelled the order to help Nishadi. TRUE / FALSE
6 Nishadi doesn't work with money any more. TRUE / FALSE

**4** **Put the events in Bắc's story in the correct order. Watch again (1:18–2:40) to check.**

___ He worked as a guard on a door.
___ He made some bodyguards angry.
___ He volunteered to work on a fundraising campaign.
___ He allowed Bill Clinton to go through the door.
___ He refused to allow Bill Clinton to go through the door.
___ He set up equipment for a conference.

**5** **Complete what Nishadi and Bắc say about their mistakes using the words in the box. Watch again to check.**

confused different gone wrong make sure not realised
not very good responsible told upset without wrong

**Nishadi**

1 I'm ______ with the UK money still, so I get a little ______.
2 I was giving out the ______ change.
3 One day I actually served a customer ______ taking money at all.
4 So I asked my manager to come and see what has ______.
5 I was really ______, so he actually took me around the store to see whether I could identify the customer.

**Bắc**

6 I was ______ for guarding a door and to ______ that no one was allowed to get in through that door.
7 I was ______ that the former president, Bill Clinton, would have got in a ______ door.
8 I had ______ that he was Bill Clinton because he looked way different from his appearance on television.

**6** **Have you got a good memory for faces? Have you ever recognised or failed to recognise a famous person?**

## GLOSSARY

**outlet** (noun): a shop that sells one type of product (in this case, fast food)
**till** (noun): the cash machine or the place in a shop where you pay
**fundraising campaign** (noun): a series of events or actions to get money (raise funds) for a particular cause
**crew** (noun): a team of people who work together

14

# In the news

**VOCABULARY**
Understanding news stories

**1** **Complete these news stories using the words in the box.**

| | | | | | |
|---|---|---|---|---|---|
| arrested | evacuated | firefighters | injured | involved | law |
| motorists | offences | oppose | police | residents | scene |

**Story 1**

1 ___________ were called out to a warehouse in Calder Street, when fire broke out there early this morning. They have now brought the fire under control, but are still at the 2 ___________ . Local 3 ___________ had to be 4 ___________ from nearby buildings, and police are advising 5 ___________ to avoid the area as the street is still closed to traffic.

**Story 2**

Two youths were 6 ___________ after a fight broke out in a night club last night. Three other people were 7 ___________ in the incident, in which one man was seriously 8 ___________. The youths were later charged with three 9 ___________ , including assault and possession of drugs.

**Story 3**

Arford City Council is planning to introduce a new 10 ___________ designed to reduce noise and disturbance in the city centre. 11 ___________ would be given powers to stop anyone making noise in the streets between the hours of 11 p.m. and 6 a.m. The Liberal party says it will 12 ___________ the new law.

**VOCABULARY**
Reacting to the news

**2** **Put the words in the correct order to complete these reactions to news stories.**

1 is / what's / that / good ______________________ health is being taken seriously.
2 that / the / thing / angry / me / makes ______________________ is that the clubs don't do more to stop these incidents.
3 thing / the / me / worries / is / that ______________________ that the bad weather is forecast to continue for another three days.
4 is / what's / funny ______________________ that there's a report in the paper at all – nothing really seems to have happened!
5 is / that / depresses / what / me ______________________ so few people went to the protest.
6 what's / is / important / that ______________________ he wasn't seriously hurt.

**3** **Match newspaper headlines a–f with the reactions (1–6) in Exercise 2.**

a **Man arrested after nightclub fight** ☐

b Peace demonstrators say no to war ☐

c Snow and ice cause havoc on roads ☐

d **Man suffers cuts and bruises in motorcycle accident** ☐

e **Smoking ban to be introduced** ☐

f Woman arrested but released without charge ☐

**Over to you**

Find some real headlines or news stories and write your reaction to them.

**GRAMMAR**
Passives

4 **Circle the correct form, active or passive, in these stories from local radio news.**

Fire [1]broke out / was broken out at a Sanders Street address last night. Firefighters [2]called / were called to the scene and the situation was soon under control. No one [3]hurt / was hurt in the fire, but the building was badly damaged.

A man has died in a diving accident. His body [4]found / was found on West Bay beach. [5]It thinks / is thought that he lost consciousness after hitting his head on an underwater rock. The man's wife [6]called / was called the police after her husband failed to return home yesterday.

And finally, the panel of judges in this year's Melton prize for children's literature [7]have announced / have been announced the winner. They [8]said / were said it was a difficult decision, but the prize [9]will give / will be given to the young writer Ben O'Keefe for his book *Angel Of The Waves*.

5 **Complete these extracts from other news stories using the correct passive form of the verbs in brackets.**

1 A woman ________________ in a motorcycle accident yesterday. (injure)
2 Over $3,000 ________________ since the charity appeal two days ago. To add your contribution, call the credit card hotline 800 300 300. (donate)
3 Scientists have made a breakthrough in the early detection of some forms of cancer. The new test can ________________ in complete safety on patients of any age. (use)
4 It ________________ that a body found yesterday in Skippers Wood is that of a man who disappeared from his home five months ago. (believe)
5 Preparations ________________ today for tomorrow's visit from the Minister for Trade and Industry. The delegation is due to arrive tomorrow morning. (make)

**VOCABULARY**
Talking about news stories

6 **Jutta and Leif are talking about a newspaper article. Circle the correct words to complete their conversation.**

**JUTTA** I [1]read / heard this interesting article [2]about / said vitamin D the other day.
**LEIF** Oh, the guy [3]what / who was saying that vitamins are actually bad for you?
**JUTTA** Yes, I [4]heard / said that, too. No, this was someone else, a Canadian doctor. Anyway, it was [5]talking / saying that vitamin D seems to prevent lots of serious diseases. Did you [6]hear / talk about that?
**LEIF** Well, I know it's good for your bones, isn't it?
**JUTTA** Yeah, but this was [7]talking / saying about things like heart disease and cancer. [8]Apparently / Obviously you get extra vitamin D from sunlight, so people in places without much sun should take loads of vitamin D supplements.
**LEIF** People like us, then!
**JUTTA** Yes, but they [9]said / read there haven't been any really big studies to prove the connection yet.

**VOCABULARY**

Evaluating and selecting

7 Three journalists on a newspaper are discussing the entries in a competition for a short piece of travel writing. Complete their conversation using the correct form (verb or adjective) of the words in the box.

convince go have got interest know look make understand want

A OK, so **this one** 1__________ **promising**.

B Yes, **it** 2__________ **potential**, I agree.

C Hmm, **I'm not** 3__________ . Personally, **I'd** 4__________ **for** this one.

A Yeah, **that sounds** 5__________ .

C **What I** 6__________ **to** 7__________ **is** if we can choose more than one winner.

A Yes, **I don't really** 8__________ that, either. Maybe we should check with the boss before we make a decision.

B Yes, **that** 9__________ **sense**. I'll call her now.

## TimeOut

8 Try this newspaper quiz.

## NEWSPAPER TRIVIA

**1** Which country is thought to have produced the first newspaper, in the 15th century?
a) Germany b) Holland c) Portugal

**2** In the 17th century, 'corantos' were small leaflets distributed when an important foreign news event occurred. In which country?
a) Spain b) France c) England

**3** The 'penny press' was the term used for the first cheaply available newspapers in the USA, and the first true form of mass media. When did these first appear?
a) the 1790s b) the 1830s c) the 1920s

**4** Which country sells the highest number of newspapers every day?
a) China b) India c) Japan

**5** Which English-language newspaper sells the highest number of copies?
a) The Times (UK) b) The New York Times c) The Times of India

**6** How many newspapers featured the comic strip, Peanuts, with the characters Charlie Brown and Snoopy?
a) over 200
b) over 1,000
c) over 2,500

# EXPLORE Writing

**9** **Read these three letters, which were written to *The Guardian* newspaper in response to an article there, and answer the questions.**

1 What was the title of the original article?
2 When did it appear in the newspaper?
3 What is the name of the journalist who wrote the article?
4 The opinion expressed in the article was that ...
   a we should travel more.
   b we should travel less.

## Our desire for unrestricted travel

**a** Simon Jenkins rightly criticises our arrogant assumption of the right to move around (*Don't blame the system for winter chaos. Stay at home*, 23 December). But first-hand knowledge of other countries is vitally important, especially for young people forming their ideas of the world. The post-war generation explored other countries cheaply and with no additional carbon footprint by hitch-hiking. Now we use transport that is expensive, both in terms of money and carbon emissions. We could start to be more open about making our cars available to hitch-hikers. Hitch-hiking can be risky, but the dangers of our young people spending their lives on the sofa are probably worse.

**Alison Prince**
*Whiting Bay, Isle of Arran*

**b** Another aspect which Simon Jenkins (23 December) does not mention is the need to support local shops. When our washing machine broke down last week, we went down to our local electrical shop at 2 p.m. By 3 p.m. a new machine was delivered and installed. Contrast that with the service you get from big chain stores.

**Andy Semple**
*Cockermouth, Cumbria*

**c** Simon Jenkins gets lots of things right when he talks about our unsocial travel habits, but he misses out the most important observation. Flexible working forces people to commute long distances. In the past, we used to move to be near our jobs. But now no one has a job for life, so everyone commutes. What a mad world. We exploit the earth and the workers at the same time.

**Chris Jeynes**
*Guildford, Surrey*

**10** Which letter ...

1 agrees with the opinion in the article and adds a reason to explain the present situation? ☐
2 partially agrees with the opinion in the article and suggests a different way of doing things? ☐
3 adds another point and makes a suggestion? ☐

**11** Which letter ends ...

1 by inviting readers to make a comparison? ☐
2 with a strong personal comment? ☐
3 with an evaluation and a preference? ☐

**12** **Write a short letter to a newspaper in response to one of the articles you read in coursebook Unit 14, or to an article you have read recently. You should:**

- give the details of the article (title, date, name of the journalist if you know it)
- say how much you agree with the writer of the article
- give your opinion or add a new point
- end your letter with a strong idea.

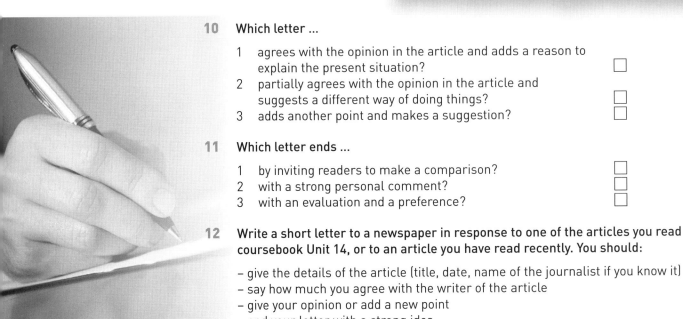

1 Before you watch, complete the information about marathons with these numbers.

3 1896 42 1921 2 500 tens 490 15

Article | Discussion | Log in/create account

The marathon is a long-distance walking or running race of just over 1_________ km. It commemorates a legendary run by an Ancient Greek messenger from the Battle of Marathon in 2_________ BC. It was one of the original events in the first modern Olympic Games in 3_________, where it was won by a Greek runner in just under 4_________ hours. The standard distance for the modern marathon was established in 5_________. More than 6_________ marathons with 7_________ of thousands of participants are now held worldwide every year. Some of the more unusual include the Great Wall of China marathon on the Great Wall itself, and the Polar Circle marathon in Greenland, run in temperatures of minus 8_________ degrees Celsius. The current records for both men and women stand at a little over 9_________ hours.

2 Watch the whole documentary about training for a marathon and tick (✓) the things Stéphane talks about.

- how he started running ☐
- why he likes running ☐
- having the right equipment ☐
- how far you should run in training ☐
- other types of exercise ☐
- how many calories you should consume daily ☐
- involving your family ☐

Stéphane

3 Watch Parts 1 and 2 again (0:06–3:07) and complete these tips for marathon training with words from the video.

## How to train for a marathon

1 Get technical advice from a ________________ club.
2 Buy some good ________________ from a running shop.
3 Allow between ________ and ________ weeks to train.
4 Include different types of activity, such as cycling or ________________, in your training.
5 ________________ before your training sessions will prepare your body for running.
6 ________________ your body after running to help it recover.

### What to include in your diet

7 ________________ and glycogens to give you ________________ for your run.
8 ________________ to be stored in reserves in your body for long-distance running.
9 A large intake of ________________ in the last few days.

**4 Stéphane explains some technical terms. Match these terms with their explanations. Watch again (0:06–3:07) to check.**

1 gait analysis
2 long run
3 repeat interval training
4 cross training
5 hitting the wall

a repeating the same exercise many times to increase your speed and strength
b when your body can't run any more because your supply of glycogen is low
c an assessment to help you run efficiently and choose the right shoes
d a regular run of 15 km or more to build up distance and stamina
e aerobic exercises like cycling which can build muscles and prevent injury

**5 Circle the correct information about the first and second time Stéphane ran the London Marathon. Watch Part 3 again (3:07–3:50) to check.**

1 His first London Marathon is his best / worst memory.
2 He was full of excitement and reached / didn't reach his target.
3 His second London Marathon is his best / worst memory.
4 He had had surgery and set his target too high / low.

**6 Complete this summary. Watch again to check.**

build up   complete overview   diet and nutrition   different sessions
good advice   intake   prevent injury   training

Marathon training gives you a 1__________ of running and training. You need to get 2__________ and buy well-fitting shoes to 3__________. Plan your 4__________ and split it into 5__________. Don't forget to include other activities besides running to 6__________ your body's ability to do exercise. Check your 7__________ and remember to keep up your 8__________ of fluid.

**7 Have you, or has anyone you know, trained or prepared for something difficult? What preparations were needed? Were they successful?**

## GLOSSARY

**carbohydrate** (noun): a substance in food such as sugar, potatoes, etc. that gives your body energy
**glycogen** (noun): a substance found in the liver and muscles which stores carbohydrate
**saturate** (verb): fill something (e.g. with a liquid) until it is completely full
**overwhelmed** (adjective): full of suddent strong emotion
**target** (noun): something that you intend to achieve